T0139280

Branching Story, Unlocked Dialogue

This book covers the distinguishing characteristics and tropes of visual novels (VNs) as choice-based games and analyzes VNs like *999: Nine Hours, Nine Persons, Nine Doors*; *Hatoful Boyfriend*; and *Monster Prom*, some of the best examples of the genre as illustrations. The author covers structuring branching narrative and plot, designing impactful and compelling choices, writing entertaining relationships and character interactions, understanding the importance of a VN's prose, and planning a VN's overall narrative design and story delivery.

The book contains exercises at the end of chapters to practice the techniques discussed. By the end of the book, if the reader finishes all the exercises, they may have several portfolio pieces or a significant portion of their own VN project designed.

Features:

- Discusses different aspects and genres of VNs, what makes them enjoyable, and successful techniques developers can incorporate into their own games
- Analyzes various VNs and choice-based games that use these successful techniques
- Shares tips from developers on portfolio pieces, hiring a team to work on VNs, and plotting and outlining VNs

Branching Story, Unlocked Dialogue: Designing and Writing Visual Novels is a valuable resource for developers and narrative designers interested in working on VNs. The book will show them how they can design their own VN projects, design branching narratives, develop entertaining plots and relationships, design impactful and compelling choices, and write prose that's a pleasure to read.

Branching Story, Unlocked Dialogue
Designing and Writing Visual Novels

Toiya Kristen Finley, PhD

CRC Press
Taylor & Francis Group
Boca Raton London New York

CRC Press is an imprint of the
Taylor & Francis Group, an **informa** business

Cover Image Credit – Character Art: Anna Strupol; Background Art: M. Azar

First Edition published 2023
by CRC Press
6000 Broken Sound Parkway NW, Suite 300, Boca Raton, FL 33487-2742

and by CRC Press
4 Park Square, Milton Park, Abingdon, Oxon, OX14 4RN

CRC Press is an imprint of Taylor & Francis Group, LLC

© 2023 Toiya Kristen Finley

Reasonable efforts have been made to publish reliable data and information, but the author and publisher cannot assume responsibility for the validity of all materials or the consequences of their use. The authors and publishers have attempted to trace the copyright holders of all material reproduced in this publication and apologize to copyright holders if permission to publish in this form has not been obtained. If any copyright material has not been acknowledged please write and let us know so we may rectify in any future reprint.

Except as permitted under U.S. Copyright Law, no part of this book may be reprinted, reproduced, transmitted, or utilized in any form by any electronic, mechanical, or other means, now known or hereafter invented, including photocopying, microfilming, and recording, or in any information storage or retrieval system, without written permission from the publishers.

For permission to photocopy or use material electronically from this work, access www.copyright.com or contact the Copyright Clearance Center, Inc. (CCC), 222 Rosewood Drive, Danvers, MA 01923, 978-750-8400. For works that are not available on CCC please contact mpkbookspermissions@tandf.co.uk

Trademark notice: Product or corporate names may be trademarks or registered trademarks and are used only for identification and explanation without intent to infringe.

Library of Congress Cataloging-in-Publication Data
Names: Finley, Toiya Kristen, author.
Title: Branching story, unlocked dialogue : designing and writing visual novels /
by Toiya Kristen Finley.
Description: Boca Raton : Taylor and Francis, 2022. |
Includes bibliographical references and index.
Identifiers: LCCN 2022025092 (print) | LCCN 2022025093 (ebook) |
ISBN 9781032059006 (hardback) | ISBN 9781032058993 (paperback) |
ISBN 9781003199724 (ebook)
Subjects: LCSH: Computer games–Programming. | Computer games–Design. |
Video games–Authorship. | Narration (Rhetoric) | Storytelling–Computer games.
Classification: LCC QA76.76.C672 F555 2022 (print) | LCC QA76.76.C672 (ebook) |
DDC 794.8/1536—dc23/eng/20220818
LC record available at https://lccn.loc.gov/2022025092
LC ebook record available at https://lccn.loc.gov/2022025093

ISBN: 978-1-032-05900-6 (hbk)
ISBN: 978-1-032-05899-3 (pbk)
ISBN: 978-1-003-19972-4 (ebk)

DOI: 10.1201/9781003199724

Typeset in Minion
by codeMantra

It's been a wild 2 years for too many reasons to count.

Thanks to Rob, Ran, Eleanor, Jules, Russell, JB, and JT for going on this VN journey with me.

Contents

Acknowledgments

M Y GRATITUDE TO ANNA Strupol, who designed the characters on the cover, and M. Azar, who illustrated the background art. Many thanks for illuminating some of the secrets contained herein!

Glossary

Archetype: Character type that frequently shows up in all storytelling media. No matter the story, these characters have similarities to other characters of the same archetype, with a particular personality, background, pattern of behavior, role in the plot, or role in relationships.

Atmosphere: The feeling or mood players sense in a scene and narrative.

Branching narrative: Nonlinear stories where the story progresses along different branches depending on player choices or other variables.

Branching structure: Types of branching narrative where the branches diverge and remerge/reconnect or do not connect in specific ways.

> **Branch and bottleneck:** A structure with nested branching and multiple endings.
>
> **Foldback structure:** Branches that all lead back to the same point.
>
> **Gauntlet:** A linear story that branches into failed endings and deaths.
>
> **Time cave:** A structure leading to multiple endings that are seemingly detached from each other because the branches never rejoin a main story.

Choice: Decisions players make to progress through the game.

> **Action choice:** What the player chooses to do.
>
> **Dialogue choice:** What the player chooses to say.

Choice-based game: Stories whose players determine their outcomes, whether those games are story-oriented or have very little story.

Computer graphic (CG): An important piece of art players unlock at a certain point in the story. CGs can also be used in cutscenes.

Conditional branch or route: Branch or route that is unlocked when the correct condition or conditions are met.

Exposition: A literary device that gives the audience necessary background information about the world and its settings, history, characters, and plot.

Gating: Locking content from the player or keeping the player from progressing because the player has not met certain requirements.

Infodump: A large amount of information given to the audience at once. The effect is that the audience feels they have a mountain of information "dumped" on them.

Love interest (LI): NPCs the player can romance.

Main character (MC): An alternate term for "player-character," most often used when referring to playable visual novel protagonists.

Mechanics: Rules players follow in order to play the game.

Metagame: Players using their external knowledge (not within the game itself) of the game or its genre(s) to determine how they will choose to play the game.

Microtransactions: Small payments for virtual goods.

Nested branches: Branching that extends off of branches.

Non-player character (NPC): Characters in the game who are not the player-character/main character.

Player agency: Players' beliefs that their actions and choices drive what happens during their gameplay sessions and impact the game.

Player-character: A game's playable protagonist.

Point of view (POV): The narrative perspective and voice the audience/player follows to understand the characters, situations, and world of the story. Usually the perspective and thoughts of a specific character.

> **First person:** In the POV character's head ("I").
>
> **Second person:** Following the POV of "you," as if the audience/player is the protagonist.
>
> **Third person limited:** "Close" to the POV character, as if looking over their shoulder ("He"/"She"/"They"/"It").
>
> **Third person omniscient:** Godlike and all-knowing POV, not hindered by time and space ("He"/"She"/"They"/"It").

Premium content: In-game content that players unlock by paying for it.

Sensory details: Descriptive writing that evokes all five senses (sight, sound, smell, touch, and taste).

Story delivery: The ways in which narrative design communicates story, world, and character through all aspects of the game, including its gameplay and mechanics, sound design, UI, etc.

Subversion: In storytelling media, the act of undermining the audience's expectations based on their knowledge of character archetypes, story tropes, fiction genres, and game genres.

Variable: A bit of stored information that the game tracks. Variables are determined by the player's choices and gameplay.

Visual novels (VN): Choice-based games with branching narrative featuring prose passages to tell their stories. Usually, they have static backgrounds and character art, or backgrounds and character art with limited animations. VNs can have a variety of mechanics.

CHAPTER 1

In Less Than 10 Years...

T HE FIRST TIME I heard the term "visual novel" was in 2010. I was at an anime convention, and I read it in the title of a talk. Intrigued, I attended the talk, a primer on visual novels (VNs). The guest discussed the popularity of VNs in Japan and how they hadn't really caught on in the United States. His educated guess was that it would take another decade before VNs found an audience in the West.

His prediction, as it turns out, was slightly off ...

I remember playing games like *Hatoful Boyfriend* and *999: Nine Hours, Nine Persons, Nine Doors* and wondering why players who loved stories didn't seem to know about VNs. At the same time, some of my friends in the industry, including writers, were declaring "Visual novels aren't games!"[1] Valve, as it turned out, had that same point of view and was not selling VNs on Steam.[2] Beyond some in the games industry's disregard for visual novels, for reasons I couldn't quite understand, VNs didn't seem to be popular in the West.

And then mobile games happened. Developers like Episode Interactive and Pixelberry Studios started publishing VNs in the mid-2010s. Suddenly, visual novels were reaching a massive audience, and many of these individuals did not consider themselves to be gamers,[3] but they enjoyed interacting with VNs. At the same time, Western indie developers were publishing their own VNs that gained loyal, dedicated fan bases. Now, thousands of VNs are on Steam, they are successful on crowdfunding platforms like Kickstarter and Indiegogo, they're available on all of the major consoles, and they make for entertaining playthroughs for content creators. In fact,

DOI: 10.1201/9781003199724-1

walkthroughs, specific scenes, and videos showing how certain games' scenarios play out tend to be popular on YouTube. It's not unusual for small accounts to have wildly successful videos featuring VNs. An account with <300 subscribers has a video for a popular visual novel with almost 412,000 views in 5 years.[4] VNs have definitely found their audience.

When KFC has the free *I Love You, Colonel Sanders!: A Finger Lickin' Good Dating Simulator* developed to sell its brand, you know VNs have gone mainstream …

Eight years after I had attended that talk, I got an editing gig working with Crazy Maple Studios and worked on VNs in their Chapters app. That same year, I wrote *Siren Song*, a visual novel for the Moments: Choose Your Story app (STARDUST). Since then, I've written VNs for NBCUniversal and Ubisoft, and served as the senior editor for Sana Stories, an app that published text-based interactive fiction. I could not have imagined that I would be working on VNs (or writing a book about them!) back in 2010.

VNs offer new developers and developers who've wanted to make their own games the opportunity to do so because they're cheaper to develop than other games. While it might be difficult to get funding, developers can pay some or all of their budget out of pocket or get their funding through crowdfunding sources. And because there's plenty of space to innovate within the genre, developers may find making VNs appealing. Diverse and marginalized voices are finding a home telling stories with VNs, and players are looking to support these indie developers.[5]

Branching Story, Unlocked Dialogue: Designing and Writing Visual Novels is a guide for developers who are looking to make visual novels, whether the VNs are their own projects, or they're working with a studio. The advice in this book is based on my years playing and analyzing visual novels, writing and editing them and other choice-based games for clients, and designing my own VN projects. I also analyze VNs and choice-based games to illustrate the design and storytelling techniques I'm sharing.

> **Part I**: Visual Novels and the VN Audience covers a brief history of visual novels, VN genres and subgenres, and the ways in which VN players engage with these stories, developers, and their own communities.

Part II: Designing and Writing Visual Novels focuses on the common elements and characteristics of VNs and how to design and write for them. Most of these chapters include exercises to practice key concepts and techniques.

You'll see a couple of icons at the beginning of these chapters, signifying whether the chapter is centered around design, writing, or both.

I've had fun working on VNs, and they've given me the freedom to play around with new mechanics and create worlds I haven't seen in other games. I hope the games featured in this book will open up design ideas to you, solve issues you may be having, and serve as inspirations for the stories you want to tell.

—TKF, May 15, 2022

NOTES

1 I'm not interested in being a gatekeeper who decides what does and does not qualify as a game. It is, honestly, an exercise that doesn't interest me.

2 Ishaan Sahdev, "How MangaGamer's Visual Novels Ended up on Steam," Siliconera, October 8, 2014, https://www.siliconera.com/how-mangagamers-visual-novels-ended-up-on-steam/.

3 Ben Tobin, "Mobile Video Game Players' Mindset: They Don't Consider Themselves 'Gamers,' Survey Finds," Phys.org, February 20, 2019, https://phys.org/news/2019-02-mobile-video-game-players-mindset.html.

4 theshydog, "What Happens If You Sleep with Robert: *Dream Daddy*," uploaded August 3, 2017, 11:09, https://www.youtube.com/watch?v=VWbrmc7a-UM.

5 Ash Treviño, "How Visual Novels Could Shape the Future of Storytelling," Screen Rant, September 27, 2021, https://screenrant.com/visual-novel-storytelling-industry-diversity-indie-game-developer/.

I

Visual Novels and the VN Audience

CHAPTER 2

Choice-Based Games and Visual Novels

THIS BOOK'S FOCUS IS on writing and designing visual novels (VNs). But, since VNs are choice-based games, much of the content will analyze and give some techniques for making *any* type of choice-based game, since visual novels use those same techniques. Before diving into exploring writing and designing VNs, let's look at choice-based games and recount a brief history of visual novels first.

WHAT ARE CHOICE-BASED GAMES?

And aren't *all* games choice-based to a certain degree? Players choose what weapons they want to use against enemies. They choose strategies for beating bosses. They decide whether to go left or right on a platform. I'm being semi-serious here, but when we talk about story in games, we often overlook that players tell their own stories in the ways that they play. Gameplay, after all, is a type of storytelling. And players use gameplay to narrate their playthroughs'[1] stories in their own imaginations. However, when I use the term **choice-based games**,[2] I'm referring to stories whose players determine their outcomes, whether those games are story-oriented or have very little story. Stories in any genre can be choice-based. They have one, a couple, or maybe all of the following mechanics and gameplay:

DOI: 10.1201/9781003199724-3

- **Choices:** The game presents two or more choices to players at certain points in the story. Choices can be **dialogue choices** that put a line of dialogue in the player-character's mouth or **action choices** where the player decides to do something, like "Take the coin" or "Trip the clown."

- **Variables:** Variables are anything in a game that can be quantified or numbered. For example, the game can keep a running count of the number of times the player jumps up on a table. Or the player's stats. Or the game can track whether the player went left or right in a level, or if the player-character has a positive, neutral, or negative relationship with a non-player character (NPC). Variables can dictate what content players do and don't see.

- **Branching Narrative:** The points at which players are given choices branch from the main story. If there are two choices at the choice point, Choice 1 diverges along one branch, and Choice 2 diverges along the other branch. Variables may also determine along which branches the story progresses, without the player having to make a choice. Each branch has its own scenario. Depending on the branch, it may have a major or minor impact on the story's plot, a character's story arc, or the player-character's relationship with one or more NPCs.

- **Multiple Endings:** Players' choices determine which ending they get during a playthrough. Games with multiple endings may only have two endings, or they can have many, many more.

Choice-Based Genres

With story gaining more importance in games over the past decade, even games that aren't choice-based offer players moments to make choices. But there are game genres that are specifically choice-based. Player expectations for these games are that their choices will change the direction of the story and determine the endings they get.

Some Choice-Based Genres[3]

Narrative Games with Choices: This is kind of a catchall name, and games that fit in this category don't fit neatly in other choice-based categories. Narrative games in general are heavily story-focused, and gameplay is sometimes at the service of the story. Some narrative games are linear without choices, but the games mentioned here have choices and multiple endings. These include *The Stanley Parable Ultra Deluxe* (Crows Crows Crows, 2022) and *Firewatch* (Campo Santo, 2016).

Adventure Games: In adventure games, players explore environments to solve puzzles and find items that will give them access to new locations and environments. Choice points, relationships with characters, and how players solve puzzles may affect how the story branches. *The Secret of Monkey Island* (LucasArts, 1990), *The Life Is Strange* franchise (DON'T NOD, 2015), and *Oxenfree* (Night School Studio, 2016) are examples.

Story-Driven RPGs: These are roleplaying games (RPGs) with RPG gameplay and mechanics, but the player influences the stories' plots, subplots, character development (sometimes for multiple characters), and endings. Story-driven RPGs include BioWare's *Mass Effect* (2007–) and *Dragon Age* (2009–) franchises, *The Witcher 3: Wild Hunt* (CD Projekt Red, 2015), *Undertale* (Toby Fox, 2015), and *Disco Elysium* (ZA/UM, 2019).

Interactive Movies/Films: There are several types of interactive movies, or several types of games that some put under the banner of "interactive movies." One type is films where the audience determines what happens next. These are shot like films or TV shows. The audience might decide choices via majority vote if it's a large group in a theater, or the audience might be a single viewer making choices with a TV remote or the user interface (UI) when watching via an online streaming service. These interactive movies include *Black Mirror: Bandersnatch* (House of Tomorrow/Netflix, 2018) and *Late Shift* (CtrlMovie, 2018).

Also under the larger banner of interactive movies are full-motion video games (FMVs), which became popular in the early and mid-1990s, and fell out of popularity in the late 1990s. The scenes of the game are made of prerecorded video files. While games like *Bandersnatch* have high production values, a great deal of the FMVs' charm is their B-movie or home video aesthetic. Classic FMVs are *Gabriel Knight* (Sierra Entertainment, 1993),

The 11th Hour (Trilobyte, 1995), and *Phantasmagoria: A Puzzle of Flesh* (Sierra Entertainment, 1996). Newer FMVs from the past decade include *Her Story* (Sam Barlow, 2015), *The Infectious Madness of Doctor Dekker* (D'Avekki Studios Limited, 2017), *Press X to Not Die* (All Seeing Eye Games, 2017), and *The Shapeshifting Detective* (D'Avekki Studios Limited, 2018).

Games with traditional art and animation assets can also be considered interactive movies or films. They're categorized as such because the mechanics tend to be limited to quick-time events (QTEs), and the focus is on story, character development, and player choice. The games "play" like being in a movie because scenes have a cinematic quality. Telltale's games including *The Walking Dead* (2012–2019) and *The Wolf among Us* (2013–) franchises, *Detroit: Become Human* (Quantic Dream, 2018), *The Dark Pictures Anthology* (Supermassive Games, 2019–), and *The Quarry* (Supermassive Games, 2022) fall under this category.

Visual Novels: VNs, as their name suggests, have the characteristics of novels. Players read passages of prose to advance the story. A common feature of VNs is limited assets (character art, background art, music, and sound effects). A hallmark of VNs is their branching structures.

THE RISE OF VISUAL NOVELS

Some classic VNs like *999: Nine Hours, Nine Persons, Nine Doors* (Spike Chunsoft Co., Ltd., 2009), the first of *The Nonary Games* stories, and *Danganronpa: Trigger Happy Havoc* (Spike Chunsoft Co., Ltd., 2010) have enjoyed new lives in remastered versions on mobile. But a few years ago, developers started making VNs specifically for the mobile medium. Most of these VNs are romance stories available in apps that act as libraries. When players finish one game, they can return to the app and find a host of others. Episode: Choose Your Story debuted in 2014,[4] Choices: Stories You Play launched in 2016,[5] and Crazy Maple Studio's Chapters: Interactive launched in 2017.[6] All three are apps with multiple VNs. In March 2022 alone, Choices made $1M USD in revenue worldwide,[7] Chapters made $2M USD,[8] and Episode made $3M USD.[9] Clearly, romance VNs have found an international audience.

A BRIEF HISTORY OF VISUAL NOVELS

The 1980s

The visual novel genre originated in Japan and did not begin to find a Western audience until recently. One of the first VNs is *Portopia Renzoku Satsujin Jiken* or *The Portopia Serial Murder Case* (1983).[10] Inspired by American adventure games, designer Yuji Horii wanted to bring story-oriented games to Japanese audiences[11]:

> I read an article in a PC magazine about a US computer game genre called 'adventure games,' which allowed players to read stories on their PCs. We still didn't have them in Japan, and I took it upon myself to make one.

The player is a detective solving the murder of an executive killed inside his mansion. The game features simple 2D environment art; text-based dialogue and prose; and choices for the player, including moving from room to room, exploring, and questioning characters.[12]

Portopia was published by Enix, and Chunsoft ported the game to the Nintendo Entertainment System (NES) in 1985.[13] Following *Portopia* was *Suishō no Dragon* or *Crystal Dragon*, a sci-fi VN set in space, developed by Square for the NES in 1986.[14] Famed *Metal Gear* franchise creator Hideo Kojima wrote *Snatcher*, which Konami released in 1988. This cyberpunk VN had "more detailed graphics, voice lines, and fully animated cutscenes."[15]

The 1990s

Snatcher received new life on the Sega CD in 1994 and was one of the only VNs of its time to be released in America.[16] Konami released *Tokimeki Memorial* in 1994. The player is a high school boy trying to romance his school girl crush. This VN's mechanics and story are "the reason why most [visual novels] adopt the dating sim/visual novel genre in hybrid form."[17] With console and PC technology improving, so did graphical capabilities. VN art evolved into a manga and anime aesthetic, with detailed characters and backgrounds. However, the narratives were still mostly linear.[18]

The 2000s

The early 2000s saw VNs evolve into games with ambitious branching narratives. *Deus Machina Demonbane* (Nitroplus, 2003) followed three main characters and their unique perspectives, and *Fate/stay night* (Type-Moon,

2004) had three routes.[19] The handheld Nintendo DS, launched in 2004, exposed international markets to VNs[20]:

> With so many people looking for unique experiences, Bateman [*999's* editor] argues that the mindset of just what a video game could be expanded with the Nintendo DS. With such a large and willing audience, Bateman contends that localization companies felt the time was right to bring over some of Japan's most popular works.

The DS introduced players to *Professor Layton and the Curious Village* (Level-5/Matrix Software, 2007),[21] *Steins;Gate* (Nitroplus/MAGE-X, 2009),[22] *Danganronpa*,[23] *999*, and *Phoenix Wright: Ace Attorney* (Capcom/Level-5, 2001).

The 2010s–

A decade ago, VNs were thought of as a niche genre among Western players. With the visual novel explosion on mobile, app users who never played games before were now playing VNs on their smartphones. (Some of these players, in fact, think of themselves as reading books, not playing games.) And Japanese VNs are now influencing Western developers. Indie developers have seen success, and their games have reached cult status. Visual novels find support on Kickstarter, including *Monster Prom* (Beautiful Glitch, 2018), which is now a series, and studio Lunaris Games has released several VNs with support from Kickstarter backers. *The Arcana: A Mystic Romance* (Nix Hydra, 2016), an indie title on mobile, has a dedicated fandom and made $70,000 USD in revenue in April 2022.[24] Because visual novels tend to have smaller budgets, VNs give indie developers the opportunity to make games with a variety of storylines and mechanics. The following are just a few Western VNs that have found fan bases and received critical acclaim: *Emily Is Away* (Kyle Seeley, 2015), *Ladykiller in a Bind* (Love Conquers All Games, 2016), *VA-11 Hall-A: Cyberpunk Bartender Action* (Sukeban Games/Poppy Works, 2016), *Doki Doki Literature Club!* (Team Salvato, 2017), *Dream Daddy: A Dad Dating Simulator* (Game Grumps, 2017), and *Murder by Numbers* (Mediatonic, 2020).

THE VERSATILITY OF VISUAL NOVELS

VNs are easier for developers, especially indies, to make games while still providing unique experiences for players because of the medium's flexibility. VNs can have both simple gameplay and presentation (player only makes choices, and there are only a few static backgrounds) or more complicated systems and assets, 3D environments, cutscenes, and every line of dialogue voiced. Like other games, VNs can also have stats, skills, and scores that the game tracks. They can include different gameplay modes, like exploration, puzzle solving, and mini games. And they incorporate the mechanics of other genres, such as hidden-object games,[25] adventure games, and RPGs.[26]

As far as story goes, VNs are perfect for any story genre or subgenre. High fantasy, slice of life, noir, space opera, romance, horror, and mystery all have a place in VNs. The diversity of stories and characters within the VN genre is something that appeals to players.

VNs are accessible to developers in terms of budget, gameplay, aesthetics, and story. Throughout the book, we'll look at how a number of visual novels and other choice-based games implement a variety of features that may be similar to the game you are designing or planning.

NOTES

1 Each distinct time of playing through a game from the beginning to the end.
2 Also known as decision-based games.
3 Sometimes games don't fit neatly in a category, and they could easily go under several of these.
4 "About Episode," Episode Interactive, accessed May 10, 2022, https://home.episodeinteractive.com/about.
5 Petrana Radulovic, "The Mobile Visual Novels Blowing up across Tumblr," Polygon, November 30, 2018, https://www.polygon.com/mobile/2018/11/30/18115080/popular-mobile-visual-novels-tumblr-video-games.
6 Erin L. Cox, "Crazy Maple Studio Introduces Chapters: Interactive Stories," Publishing Perspectives, November 14, 2017, https://publishingperspectives.com/2017/11/crazy-maple-studio-introduces-chapters-interactive-stories/.
7 "Choices: Storie You Play," Sensor Tower, accessed May 10, 2022, https://app.sensortower.com/ios/us/pixelberry-studios/app/choices-stories-you-play/1071310449/overview.
8 "Chapters: Interactive Stories," Sensor Tower, accessed May 10, 2022, https://app.sensortower.com/android/US/crazy-maple-studio-dev/app/chapters-interactive-stories/com.mars.avgchapters/overview.
9 "Episode: Choose Your Story," Sensor Tower, accessed May 10, 2022, https://app.sensortower.com/ios/US/episode-interactive/app/episode-choose-your-story/656971078/overview.
10 Some would dispute, and some would support, whether it is indeed the first.
11 "Portopia Renzoku Satsujin Jiken," *Retro Gamer*, https://2.bp.blogspot.com/_kGAOBLrWIr4/TUgMtkSB28I/AAAAAAAACyk/oj3PBRY70HM/s1600/DSC01599.JPG.

12 "Portopia Renzoku Satsujin Jiken," The Visual Novel Database, accessed May 11, 2022, https://vndb.org/v4511.

13 Katerina Bashova and Veno Pachovski, "Visual Novel" (paper presented at ICT Innovations, September 2013), https://www.researchgate.net/publication/306083425_Visual_novel.

14 Cecil Choi, "Bigger on the Inside: A History of Visual Novels," *Medium* (blog), February 22, 2019, https://medium.com/@cecilchoi/bigger-on-the-inside-a-history-of-visual-novels-981e42f43608.

15 Ibid.

16 Ibid.

17 Mr. Toffee, "This Classic 90s Visual Novel Is Finally Out in English for the First Time," Kakuchopurei, March 7, 2022, https://www.kakuchopurei.com/2022/03/this-classic-90s-visual-novel-is-finally-out-in-english-for-the-first-time/.

18 Pete Davison, "The Three Ages of Visual Novels," Moegamer.net, September 29, 2017, https://moegamer.net/2017/09/28/the-three-ages-of-visual-novels/.

19 Ibid.

20 Tyler Ohlew, "Text Adventures: The Story of Visual Novels in America," USgamer, September 6, 2014, https://www.usgamer.net/articles/visual-novels-in-america.

21 Tyler Ohlew, "Text Adventures: The Story of Visual Novels in America," USgamer, September 6, 2014, https://www.usgamer.net/articles/visual-novels-in-america.

22 Tyler Ohlew, "Text Adventures: The Story of Visual Novels in America," USgamer, September 6, 2014, https://www.usgamer.net/articles/visual-novels-in-america.

23 Tyler Ohlew, "Text Adventures: The Story of Visual Novels in America," USgamer, September 6, 2014, https://www.usgamer.net/articles/visual-novels-in-america.

24 "The Arcana: A Mystic Romance," Sensor Tower, accessed May 10, 2022, https://app.sensortower.com/ios/us/nix-hydra-games/app/the-arcana-a-mystic-romance/1165696961/overview.

25 Players look for objects hidden within the art of a scene.

26 In role-playing games (RPGs), players level up their characters by gaining experience and choosing skills and abilities for their characters to level up and master.

CHAPTER 3

Visual Novel Genres and Platforms

VNs CAN FALL INTO more than one genre or subgenre or be on more than one platform. Over the past decade, visual novels have been published on a variety of platforms: PC, handheld consoles, consoles, web only, and mobile. It's good to think about your VN's genres and/or subgenres in relation to marketing the game because it can fit into an established category with an audience of players who enjoy that genre.

Visual novel genres are evolving as developers in both the East and West put their own spins on them and their audiences change and grow.

KINETIC

Kinetic visual novels are different from other VNs in that they don't have any branching or choices. There's one linear plot. They do include other characteristics of visual novels, like art and audio.

Examples:

Higurashi When They Cry (07th Expansion/Alchemist, 2007)

Highway Blossoms (Studio Élan/Studio Coattails, 2016)

The Fountain (Jeanne Foissard, 2018)

DOI: 10.1201/9781003199724-4

HYBRID/GAMES WITH VN ELEMENTS

Some games in other genres use the story-delivery methods of visual novels. These games have traditional VN features, like character sprites that face the player during conversations, text boxes and narration, dialogue and action choices, and branching narrative. These storytelling features accompany gameplay from other genres, like action adventure, strategy, RPG, and simulation.

Examples:

Persona franchise (Atlus, 1996–)

Ace Attorney franchise (Level-5/Capcom, 2001–)

The Nonary Games (Spike Chunsoft Co., Ltd., Chime, 2009–2016)

Pyre (Supergiant Games, 2017)

ROMANCE SUBGENRES

The focus of a lot of VN stories is romance, or the VN has romance elements and routes where players can romance the NPCs of their fantasies. In recent years, VNs with romantic stories have flourished on mobile.[1]

Romance VN genres have specific audiences that they cater to. These subgenres were established in Japan, and Western developers are now making VNs with these tropes or expanding the audiences for these subgenres. While a lot of Western VNs have manga and anime art styles, which are traditional in Japan, other games are moving away from that aesthetic.

Otome

The *otome* subgenre owes its existence to Keiko Erikawa. Erikawa believed there needed to be more opportunities for women in game development, so she founded the all-female team, Ruby Party, at Koei (later Koei Tecmo) in 1990.[2] Ruby Party's first game (and the first game targeting an all-female audience) was *Angelique*, released on the Super Nintendo Entertainment System.[3]

Otome feature female protagonists with male LIs (love interests), and the original target audience was young female players in Japan.[4] Common settings for these games are "high school, college, or some sort of magic school."[5] In the West, otome games have found both female and queer audiences. Players can choose their character's gender and pronouns, and they can romance characters of more than one gender.[6]

Examples:

Mystic Messenger (Cheritz, 2016–)

LongStory: Choose Your Date (Bloom Digital, 2014–)

Hatoful Boyfriend: A School of Hope and White Wings (Hato Moa/ Mediatonic/Devolver Digital, 2014)

Bishoujo

Bishoujo (also *bishojo*) games ("girl games"), and their subgenre *eroge*, got their start in the 1980s[7] and are for heterosexual male audiences, with female LIs. These were the first of the Japanese romance VNs and dating sims to be localized in the West, and they are the most frequently translated and released in English.[8] The genre began due to competition between Japanese PC manufactures. NEC's PC-9801 had weaker hardware, so it promoted porn games for men, or *eroge*, to attract customers. The first *eroge*, *Night Life*, was published by Koei in 1982.[9]

In *bishoujo* scenarios, "the main goal is to interact with cute animelike girls," and in some games, scenes "tend to be more suggestive, featuring romantic or sexy situations."[10] This does not, however, mean that the suggestive cannot be raunchy or centered around sexualized themes.[11] Like *eroge*, some *bishoujo* is quite explicit.

The protagonist archetype tends to be a faceless cipher, and LI archetypes fall into categories like *tsundere*, *yandere*, and childhood friend. (For more on character archetypes, see "Writing MCs and NPCs: Character Development and Routes.")

Examples:

Tokimeki Memorial (Konami, 1994)

Fate/stay night (Type-Moon, 2004)

Doki Doki Literature Club! (Team Salvato, 2017)

Boys' Love/Yaoi

In Japan, boys' love (BL) or *yaoi* media feature gay male romances for female audiences. BL games have evolved in the West to mean games focusing on male/male romances in general.[12] The protagonist is a young, attractive man seeking attractive LIs; the romance is "idealized 'pure love' and dynamic relationships that aren't bound by societal norms"; and the characters tend to fall into roles in their relationships: *seme* (the dominant) and *uke* (the receptive).[13] Unlike in *bishoujo* games, the protagonist is a defined and fleshed-out character, and games can be PG-rated or more explicit.[14] Women are entertained by the genre for several reasons, including hot guy-on-guy action, the voyeuristic element of cis straight women peering into the lives of queer men and boys, "a desire for a 'truly equal' partnership that the fans do not believe they'll get in a male/female romance or sex (due to sexism, inequality, patriarchy, etc.),"[15] and the opportunity for players to explore their own sexuality.[16]

In Japan, the aesthetic for LIs is *bishounen* ("beautiful boy"), and they're "drawn as at least partially androgynous. Long hair, elegant features, willowy bodies, and graceful poses are par for the course, with any 'rugged' male love interests usually in the minority as an exception to the rule."[17] In the West, the LIs are drawn with more Western ideals of handsome or beautiful.

Examples:

DRAMAtical Murder (Nitro+chiral, 2012)

Dream Daddy: A Dad Dating Simulator (Game Grumps, 2017)

Chess of Blades (Argent Games, 2017)

Yuri

Yuri are games featuring lesbian romances. *Yuri's* roots originated in anime and manga, and its target audience was queer women. Stories focus on intimate relationships between young women, "not just sexual and romantic, but along other social lines as well, and often blurring and conflating the lines between the two, often resulting in what could be best termed as 'romantic friendships.'"[18]

The audience for *yuri* are both male and female players, with certain games targeting female players, and vice versa. The purposes of stories range from straight-male titillation to queer expression to queer fantasy.[19]

Examples:

Analogue: A Hate Story (Christine Love, 2012)

Kindred Spirits on the Roof (Liar-soft, 2012)

Contract Demon (NomnomNami, 2019)

Bara

Bara games are gay romances for gay male audiences, mostly made by queer men.[20] *Bara's* audience is different than *yaoi's*, as it focuses on "muscle love,"[21] and characters do not fall into the *uke* and *seme* roles.[22] Characters are[23]

> Very masculine … with significant (though often realistic) levels of musculature, body fat, and body hair. Beards and potbellies are common, as are heavy emphasis on hairy arms, chests, etc. This would correspond somewhat with the Western idea of 'bears' in the gay community.

Most games take place in contemporary, real-world settings, as games explore gay male life.[24]

As is the case with other subgenres, the audiences for *bara* are not as well defined as they used to be. Western audiences make up queer men and women, and *Coming Out on Top*, with "explicit sexual scenes and heavily muscled, hairy, and overweight male characters," was created by a straight cisgender woman.[25]

Examples:

Coming Out on Top (Obscurasoft, 2014)

Let's Meat Adam (SoulsoftEA, 2017)

Alpha Hole Prison (Y Press Games, 2021)

STAT RAISING

How the game branches and/or whom the main character (MC)[26] can romance or befriend is based upon their stats because LIs are attracted to certain stats (personality/character attributes). This means there are grinding elements, like visiting a particular location repeatedly or doing a certain task over and over in order to increase stats associated with the location or task. Of course, if players can increase their stats, they can also experience decreased stats when failing a stat check. In *Monster Prom*, for example, players always have two choices during events. Each choice is a stat check. If their stats aren't high enough for a choice, the player will fail, and one or more of their stats will be decreased.

The grinding nature of stat raisers can be frustrating, as this type of gameplay exhausts a lot of players. The repetition of doing the same job or task or visiting the same location can also bore players if they receive the same text over and over, and there's no new dialogue or narration to break up the monotony:[27]

> … all you do is choose an activity with the same results each time and no real influence except for your stat of choice to go up by X. I feel like I'm forcing myself through those parts to get to the plot which lies behind them.

If players are trying to get certain outcomes and they need stats to be high enough, the wait is not worth the eventual reward.

One way *Monster Prom* gets around the frustrating part of grinding is by following up visiting the location and increasing the stat with an event featuring one or more LIs. The story is always progressing, even as players grind. *Hatoful Boyfriend: A School of Hope and White Wings* has a similar mechanic where the MC goes to certain classes to increase stats in vitality, charisma, and wisdom. LIs attend specific classes, as well. So, going to a class not only ups certain stats, but it is also a way for players to spend time with their preferred LIs.

Other Examples:

1931: Scheherazade at the Library of Pergamum (Black Chicken Studios, 2012)

Backstage Pass (sakevisual, 2016)

Royal Alchemist (Nifty Visuals, 2020)

DATING SIMS

While dating sims are a subgenre of simulation games, quite a few of them use visual novels' storytelling techniques and aesthetics. Similar to stat raisers, dating sims present players with LIs whom they can develop relationships with. Players often must increase skills to attract LIs and maintain good relationships with them. These games also have a time management mechanic,[28] where players must decide what activities they will complete and which locations they will visit in a day. What they do and where they go also have effects on relationships and which LIs they can date in a playthrough.

Examples:

Sakura Wars franchise (Sega, 1996–)

My Horse Prince (Usaya, 2016–2020)

I Love You, Colonel Sanders!: A Finger Lickin' Good Dating Simulator (KFC/Psyop, 2019)

MOBILE VNS

Apps like Choices: Stories You Play and Chapters: Interactive Stories are libraries housing multiple episodic visual novels. (Developers may also refer to their VNs as "books.") These are **free-to-play (F2P)** games, meaning players can experience much of a game's content without having to pay for it. Players can pay **microtransactions** for the rest of a F2P game's content. Microtransactions (small payments for virtual goods) in choice-based games give players access to premium choices, which lead to special scenes, longer interactions with NPCs, and even relationship boosts with some characters. STARDUST'S Moments: Choose Your Story app (2018–) has an additional feature with paper-doll mechanics: each reader has their own virtual room where they can buy outfits to wear and place in them the avatars of characters from the stories they've played. The more popular or in demand characters are, the more difficult it is to get their avatars (in other words, players unlock them by reading most of the game's chapters or the entire game). Writers and designers should take care to design premium choices and content that players will want to pay for. (For more on designing premium content, please see "Writing for VN and Other Choice-Based Apps.")

Games in visual novel apps tend to be published in installments. Depending on the developer, they refer to these as "chapters" or "episodes."

Standalone visual novels are also published on mobile. These are more traditional VNs where players pay for the game once, and there are no premium choices to be paid for by microtransactions.

Because these visual novels are released on mobile, developers design them with shorter play sessions in mind. Chapters or installments are meant to be played in a few minutes, and narrative passages and dialogue are shorter in comparison to non-mobile VNs.

Classic visual novels released on older consoles have also been remastered for mobile, like *999: Nine Hours, Nine Persons, Nine Doors* (originally released on the Nintendo DS).

Examples:

Episode app (Pocket Gems, Inc., 2014)

The Arcana: A Mystic Romance (Nix Hydra, 2016–)

Underworld Office (Buff Studio, 2020)

NOTES

1 Thanks to Michelle Clough, an expert on romance and sexuality in games, who gave me insight into most of this section's content.
2 Anne Lee, "The Story Behind the All-Woman Team Who Invented the Otome Genre," Waypoint, March 1, 2018, https://www.vice.com/en/article/d3wjpv/all-woman-team-otome-angelique-ruby-party.
3 Xiaolan You, "Otome Games: Character and Plot Tropes in Japanese Otome Games," Unsuitable, accessed April 5, 2022, https://sites.duke.edu/unsuitable/otome-games/.
4 Michelle Clough, message to author, April 28, 2022.
5 Ibid.
6 Ibid.
7 Ana Matilde Sousa, "The Screen Turns You on: Lust for Hyperflatness in Japanese 'Girl Games,'" in *Post-Screen: Device, Medium and Concept*, Helena Ferreira and Ana Vicente (eds). (Lisbon: CIEBA-FBAUL, 2014), 238–248.
8 Michelle Clough, message to author, April 28, 2022.
9 Ana Matilde Sousa, "The Screen Turns You on: Lust for Hyperflatness in Japanese 'Girl Games,'" in *Post-Screen: Device, Medium and Concept*, Helena Ferreira and Ana Vicente (eds). (Lisbon: CIEBA-FBAUL, 2014), 238–248.
10 Jean Snow, "Video: *Bishoujo* Games for the Summer," Wired, May 30, 2008, https://www.wired.com/2008/05/bishojo-games-f/.
11 Michelle Clough, message to author, April 28, 2022.
12 Ibid.
13 Huann Binimbol, "What Is Boys' Love (BL)?" Manga Planet, April 3, 2020, https://mangaplanet.com/what-is-boys-love/.
14 Michelle Clough, message to author, April 28, 2022.
15 Ibid.
16 Huann Binimbol, "What Is Boys' Love (BL)?" Manga Planet, April 3, 2020, https://mangaplanet.com/what-is-boys-love/.
17 Michelle Clough, message to author, April 28, 2022.
18 Ibid.

19 Ibid.
20 Ibid.
21 Tina Anderson, "That Damn Bara Article!" *GGY Meta* (blog), accessed May 12, 2002, https://web.archive.org/web/20090327212637/http://ggymeta. wordpress.com/popular-gay-manga-posts/that-bara-article/.
22 Huann Binimbol, "What Is Boys' Love (BL)?" Manga Planet, April 3, 2020, https://mangaplanet.com/what-is-boys-love/.
23 Michelle Clough, message to author, April 28, 2022.
24 Ibid.
25 Ibid.
26 In visual novels, the player-character is more commonly called the main character or MC.
27 Anna, "Re: What's fun in a stat-raising sim?", Lemma Soft Forums, December 18, 2011, https://lemmasoft.renai.us/forums/viewtopic.php?t=13059.
28 Mechanics, established through a game's design, are the rules players follow in order to play the game. For example, in platformers, jumping is a mechanic. In adventure games, solving puzzles and pixel hunting are mechanics. A game may have one or many mechanics.

CHAPTER 4

The Visual Novel Audience

NO MATTER THE GENRE, games will have their passionate fan bases. Players will have expectations for every genre. With platformers, players expect there to be jumping mechanics. In role-playing games (RPGs), they expect to be able to pick a character class and customize their player-character's skills, etc. Visual novel (VN) players also have expectations for VNs, and there are some unique ways in which they interact with and experience VNs.

While these player expectations and interactions won't necessarily be the driving forces for your writing and design, you do want to be aware of them. When you keep these expectations and interactions in mind, they can help you enhance your game, make it a more enjoyable experience, and avoid certain pitfalls about VNs that frustrate players.

VN players can get passionate about their favorite characters and storylines/arcs (routes). Here are some ways players perceive and interact with VNs.

READING IS *GOOD*!

One of the first things you might have to do when approaching working on a VN is to adjust your thinking about how players digest the story. The story bits can be some of the most frustrating parts of a game for players. From their perspectives, cutscenes and dialogue *interrupt* their gameplay experiences. As narrative designers and game writers, we know that our

DOI: 10.1201/9781003199724-5

lovingly crafted words might be ignored or never be seen or heard, thanks to the ubiquitous "Skip" button. There is nothing wrong with players wanting to avoid the talky parts—sometimes, players aren't in it for the story.

However, the very nature of VNs is that there's lots of text. Text helps to move the game forward. With limited assets in VNs and some other choice-based games, text describes what the world looks like, explains sounds in the scene, and even communicates the emotions and expressions on characters' faces. These are *novels* after all, and the reading is a pleasurable part of playing a VN.

Think of all of the different styles of prose writing. You can begin to imagine the myriad narrative voices you can dream up for a VN. If you're not as experienced writing prose fiction, don't worry. We'll talk about prose writing techniques in "The 'Novel' Part of 'Visual Novel': Perfecting Prose."

THE ROLE OF METAGAMING IN THE PLAYER'S EXPERIENCE

Most VNs have multiple endings. They usually have a couple of routes specific to non-player characters (NPCs) and/or love interests that players come to care about, and they have unlockables, like CGs.[1] This creates an "explore and discover" relationship between the VN and the player. We usually consider exploration as a feature of games where players can move around in environments or pixel hunt.[2] A lot of visual novels don't have point-and-click features or controls that allow players free movement in an environment or scene. But that doesn't mean that VN players can't explore.

Players can explore in several ways:

Return to a Scene Multiple Times: This repetition can lead to an NPC unexpectedly showing up the fourth or fifth time or unlocking new dialogue or narration.

Exhaust Dialogue Trees: If the player tries every dialogue choice in the tree, they might get bonus dialogue.

Befriend Certain NPCs and Antagonize Others: Relationships are significant factors to the parts of the story players can and can't unlock. If NPCs are rivals, that means one of them will sour on the player if the player chooses to get friendlier with their enemy. So, the player will see different sides of NPCs, get different dialogue, and have different dialogue choices based on how NPCs feel about them.

Acquire Different Stats: Some visual novels and choice-based games do have stats. Specific stats (and specific stats at particular values) give players access to certain locations, relationships with NPCs, story arcs, choices, etc.

Play the Game Several Times: Players aren't able to make every choice, see every narrative branch, or unlock every route when they play for the first time. Sometimes, it takes several playthroughs to experience everything in the game (similar to other types of games).

Exploration in visual novels is akin to players figuring out what combinations they need to get their desired outcomes. *How high does my humor stat need to be to unlock the true ending? Do I need to piss off Sven to get to Mabel's route? Do I need to go back to the diner and talk to FaVR to get access to the underground cavern, which unlocks the Devastate Ending?* This is how players metagame[3] in visual novels. Entire communities on sites like Steam, Discord, and Reddit center themselves around metagaming and helping each other find secrets in visual novels and provide walkthroughs.

Getting All of the Endings

Monster Prom tracks the new content players unlock. At the end of each session, the game reports these stats. The content tracked includes new secret endings, new events, new outcomes, and the number of events, endings, and outcomes the player has unlocked vs. the total number of events, endings, and outcomes. This information not only reports to players what new content they've experienced, but it also encourages them to keep playing and seeing if they can get new endings (secret and otherwise) and new events. The game literally says, "You have unlocked 29 of 1384 outcomes."

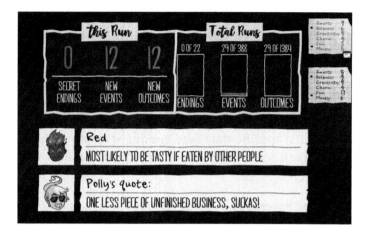

CAPTION: Screenshot from the end of a *Monster Prom* playthrough. Developed by Beautiful Glitch and protected by United States and international copyright law. © Beautiful Glitch.
Jeanne Tan, "Geek Review: *Monster Prom*," Geek Culture, April 20, 2018, https://geekculture.co/geek-review-monster-prom/.

Communicating directly to players in this way about what they have and haven't seen is a smart way to say, "Hey, keep playing! There's a lot left for you to discover." Other visual novels do something similar, in that they tell players

CAPTION: *Hatoful Boyfriend* titles and numbers endings. Developed by Hato Moa, Mediatonic, and Devolver Digital and protected by United States and international copyright law. © Mediatonic. PressHearttoContinue.
"*HATOFUL BOYFRIEND*: Part 3 NAGEKI ENDING: I Promised I Wouldn't Cry …," uploaded September 13, 2014, YouTube video, 28:39, https://www.youtube.com/watch?v=KTohev37ysQ.

the total number of endings in the game and which ending the player has just unlocked: "You have unlocked ending 4 of 6." Or they give each ending a number and let the player try to figure out how many there are in total.

Another tactic is for the game to show the players an in-game flowchart of all possible branches and routes *during* a playthrough. These flowcharts signal that there is content they're not seeing, and they will have to play again to unlock it.

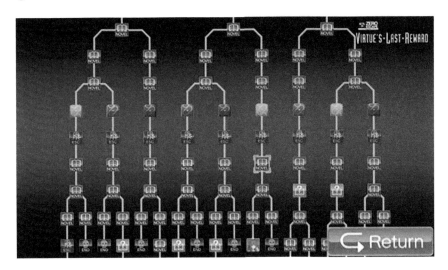

CAPTION: *Zero Escape: Virtue's Last Reward's* (the second game in *The Nonary Games* series) in-game flowchart. In-game flowcharts are a main gameplay and narrative element of *The Nonary Games* because the flowcharts hint at what choices players can make to unlock more of the story or show them what parts of the story and branches they've already seen. Developed by Spike Chunsoft and protected by United States and international copyright law. © Spike Chunsoft Co., Ltd.
Christian Nutt, "The Storytelling Secrets of *Virtue's Last Reward*," Game Developer, January 11, 2013, https://www.gamedeveloper.com/design/the-storytelling-secrets-of-i-virtue-s-last-reward-i-.

Some developers will directly encourage their players and tell them how to find endings. Episodes Interactive, a mobile VN publisher, puts on its Instagram account information on how to get secret endings.[4] I did something similar to this with my VN for Moments. *Siren Song* has seven endings; a couple are almost impossible to get (there are several choices the player has to make throughout the story, including one premium one early on). As soon as the last chapter released, I posted in the story's chat that there were seven endings. Seven months later, players were still asking how to get that super difficult ending.

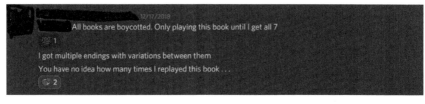

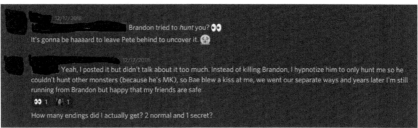

CAPTION: Players share endings they've gotten and try to help each other find all of the *Siren Song* endings.

After a lot of player discussion on how to get the most difficult ending (and a lot of replays trying to get it!), I eventually shared in a fan Discord server the choices they needed to make over the VN's 15 chapters.

CAPTION: The steps for getting one of *Siren Song's* secret endings.

Figuring Out Who the LIs Are

CAPTION: Pete was not, alas, available for romance.

Some dating sims use the storytelling features of visual novels. One of the most fun things about these dating sims for players is discovering who the romanceable NPCs are. Sometimes, it's obvious who the LIs are. A common trope the story uses introduces them to the MC as if shining a giant light on them: "YOU CAN ROMANCE THIS CHARACTER, OKAY?" There are different ways of doing this. The MC might note how attracted they are to the character in their thoughts. The story introduces players to all of the LIs near the start of the story, so the player can start thinking about whom they wish to romance. Or there are other cues the game uses. In *Hatoful Boyfriend: A School of Hope and White Wings*, for instance, the game presents the player with both the images of the potential bird boyfriends and the human imaginings of them when the MC first talks to them.

CAPTION: Anghel Higure and his human likeness, *Hatoful Boyfriend: A School of Hope and White Wings*. Developed by Hato Moa, Mediatonic, and Devolver Digital and protected by United States and international copyright law. © Mediatonic.
"Anghel Higure," *Hatoful Boyfriend* Wiki, accessed May 14, 2022, https://hatoful. fandom.com/wiki/Anghel_Higure.

But it's fun for players to figure out who the LIs are when the visual novel doesn't signal this. It's also fun for them to suss out how to romance difficult LIs. For "regular" LIs, players can intuit their likes and dislikes, spend more time with them than other characters, give them gifts, and/ or build up certain stats/traits that the LI finds attractive. However, while these tactics may or may not work with "hard to get" LIs, there are a couple (or several) more things the player needs to do (or to *avoid*) to win the hearts of difficult LIs. We'll do a deeper dive into designing LI routes in "Writing MCs and NPCs: Character Development and Routes."

PERCEPTIONS OF THE WRITING AND WRITER

At the beginning of this chapter, I mentioned that reading is something that VN players look forward to. Because the writing is a highlight, this means that the *writer(s)* is also in the spotlight. In other games, while players might enjoy the story and writing, they may not know the identities of the writers or think about the fact that there's a narrative team. Visual novel players, however, are very aware of the story and its writing, and they may know exactly who the writer is. Some mobile apps publish the names of their visual novel writers. Again, in this way, the visual novel audience is more akin to an audience who follows a novelist, comics writer, or *mangaka*.[5]

The spotlight on both writing and writer has its benefits and disadvantages. Players loving a story and its characters is its own reward. However, when players *don't* like something, it's easier for them to be more critical of the writer than if they were playing other types of games. In other types of games, they might be annoyed with the story, or they might not even like it, but there might be other aspects of the game that they enjoy. They can shrug off the story. Or, if they don't like the game, there are several things about it they don't enjoy that they can point to. If players don't like the music, art, or story in a visual novel, their focus is likely going to be more on the writing than anything else.

Sometimes, this is just an issue of taste. The game might be well received by some players but disliked by others. That's just something writers have to deal with all of the time, everywhere, no matter the medium. But there *are* writing issues for visual novels that are legitimate complaints from players, and there are things we can do to avoid them.

In stories where there are multiple LIs, players get frustrated when they feel the writer has a "canon" or "preferred" love interest, or that the writer treats certain NPCs unfairly. In other words, they perceive that the writer is playing favorites. It comes through in the story that the writer enjoys some NPCs over others. There's an "implied" love interest—the one the writer believes players should choose. There are NPCs that the writer likes more than others, and the characters the player likes are ignored or not given enough screen time. Players can feel a similar way about endings. Their favorite ending is not the writer's, and they feel their ending has been given short shrift. As the writer, you may *not* be playing favorites or punishing players with certain endings, and you certainly aren't intentionally inferring that there are right and wrong LIs to romance. However, everyone has biases (you can certainly have your favorite characters in stories you write), but you don't want that to be evident in your writing.

Player agency is just as important a concept in visual novels as it is in other games. Players should have some control over what happens in the game (and the story). To some extent, this is illusory, because players can't do *everything* they want or change some aspects of the story. However, what they *are* able to do should feel impactful, and that they are the driving influence as to what happens. If there is obvious bias (or perceived bias) from the writer, then the player loses that sense of control. The story doesn't treat their favorite characters as they would wish for them to be treated. The story (and the writer) is passing judgment on their tastes and desires and what they enjoy. Again, all of this may simply be *perceived*. Players love their stories and their characters, and they can passionately express their displeasure. While you can't please everyone, there are certain things you can do to make your stories balanced. We'll look at these in "Choices, Variables, and Relationships: Designing Branching Narratives" and "Writing MCs and NPCs: Character Development and Routes."

NONTRADITIONAL WAYS PLAYERS INTERACT WITH VNs

Visual novels' limited assets provide opportunities for players to engage with their content in ways other game genres don't. While some VNs are voiced, most are not, or only parts are voiced. Additionally, there's plenty of text, whether that's narration, descriptions, journal entries, etc. If you've watched Twitch or YouTube streamers play VNs, you've probably witnessed them read all of the text and create different voices for the characters. In comments, viewers will often say, "Your version of this character is canon for me." Sometimes, streamers will invite friends to help perform the multiple characters and aid them in deciding which choices to make. It's fun for both the streamers and their audiences to listen to them "get into character" or interact with friends if more than one streamer is playing along. Multiple streamers' interpretations of characters give fans of the streamers and players of the game several ways to experience the game and characters over and over.

Players may not be streaming. Friends get together, dole out parts, and take turns when it's their time to act out their character. I have spent several evenings with friends at conventions divvying up parts to play *Monster Prom* characters, for instance.

Unless there are portions of the VN that are voiced, you're not necessarily writing with the text being voiced in mind. However, you can think about making the writing fun to read aloud or give readers provocative moments to add their own emotional inflections. Because a voice actor won't be performing the dialogue, you can write in more of an accent or dialect or make the tone over the top. (These are things you would avoid for voiced dialogue. Overexaggerated dialogue could lead to stereotyped and caricatured performances, when you want the actor to bring their own nuances to the performance instead.)

ENGAGE YOUR AUDIENCE!

"Engage your audience" might seem like advice that does not need to be given. The point of any game is to be engaging. However, since metagaming is a part of the *culture* of VN players, you can always write and design knowing that players will be involved in some level of metagaming. This doesn't mean that you have to *force* into your design elements that will inspire players to metagame. However, if your game has multiple endings, as an example, naming or numbering them would encourage players to find them all.

NOTES

1 Short for "computer graphic." These are images, usually illustrations, unlocked during playthroughs.
2 Using a cursor to scan the environment to find interactable items and art. It's a "pixel hunt" because some of these interactables are intentionally hard to find, and the player has to touch the right pixel or small grouping of pixels.
3 How players use their external knowledge (not within the game itself) of the game or its genre(s) to determine how they will choose to play the game. For example, players will know that the childhood friend is someone they can romance before it's revealed in the story, and they will try to figure out how to romance that character from the start of the game. This knowledge of the childhood friend comes from playing lots of games with the archetypal romanceable childhood friend.
4 Cass Phillips, "All Choice No Consequence: Efficiently Branching Narrative," Game Developers Conference 2016, YouTube video, 30:14, https://www.youtube.com/watch?v=TEa9aSDHawA.
5 An artist and/or writer of manga.

II

Designing and Writing Visual Novels

Mileage always varies on how many years you can wait before discussing spoilers. Before I proceed, I should note that there will be pretty significant spoilers in some of the book's game analyses.

Please read on with caution.

CAPTION: Artist Unknown

DOI: 10.1201/9781003199724-6

CHAPTER 5

The Story Delivery of Visual Novels

THE ASSETS APPEARING ON the VN screen narrate the game's story in a simple but effective way. Contrast these to other game genres where there might be multiple menus, buttons, meters, a heads-up display (HUD), and more than one text box on the screen at once, and it may take a while for the player to get used to everything in front of them. Even for those who have never played a visual novel (VN), they can quickly understand what all of the storytelling elements on the screen are communicating to them.

As I mentioned in "In Less Than 10 Years …," VN tropes and storytelling techniques work with any game genre or story genre. In this chapter, I'll analyze the most common features of VNs' story delivery, its narrative design, and why they're so accessible to players.

WHAT IS STORY DELIVERY?

Simply put, **story delivery** is part of **narrative design**, which uses all aspects of the game, creative and technical, for storytelling and world-building. Story delivery isn't what we think of as traditional aspects of

DOI: 10.1201/9781003199724-7

37

the story (plot, characters, worldbuilding, dialogue), but the techniques by which we communicate those traditional aspects of the story in every part of the game.

Narrative design ensures that the world, story, and characters are reflected in all parts of the game and that the story elements of the game embody gameplay. It makes sure that all parts of a game are used to tell the story. So, if the story is dark and moody, those dark and moody themes are in the game's music. If the story is set in a utopia, the environments feature bright, sunny days; state-of-the-art architecture; and vibrant, blue water. If the world is in a fantasy setting, the user interface (UI) design and menus have what we might think of as features of ancient, magical books: filigreed edges and gilded gold overlays.

When I was thinking about the look of *Incarnō: Everything Is Written's* UI, I wanted it to reflect the importance of the book that features prominently in the story. *Incarnō* is not only the name of the VN series, but it is also a book of unknown origin. The goal of the book's art is for one to be able to tell that it's powerful and magical just by looking at it. The UI for *Incarnō: Everything Is Written* echoes details from *Incarnō* the physical book.

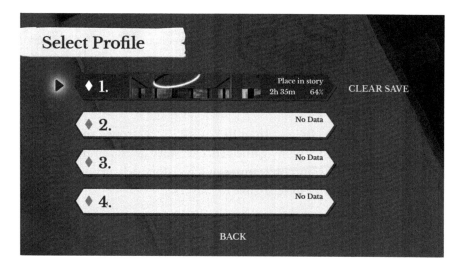

CAPTION: The book appears in the background of *Incarnō's* save menu. The design includes details evocative of symbols and illustrative flourishes found in the book. UI design by Jules Riseling. Developed by Schnoodle Studio and protected by United States and international copyright law. © Schnoodle Studio.

With narrative design's story delivery, every aspect of the game communicates to players something about the story, characters, and world. VN screens have several common features that deliver story.

UI

The UI has a prominent place in a VN's story delivery. Players constantly interact with it. They tap on or click text boxes to advance narration or dialogue or make choices. They save their games or view art they've unlocked in galleries through the UI. And, if the VN includes it, players can view a story and choose a flowchart that shows them what routes they've unlocked and branches of the story they've not yet seen.

Below are more in-depth looks at the UI's story elements: text boxes. Some VNs use one text box for all the different types of text in the games. However, you might consider having text box designs if it's in your budget. The *look* of each text box can say a lot about its function and can help players tell the difference between, say, narration and dialogue.

Narration Text Box

VNs are a lot like prose fiction in that narration is prominent in their writing. (For more on the role of narration, please see "The 'Novel' Part

CAPTION: The MC narrates their actions, which they describe as "blink[ing] unnaturally." Screenshot from *Errant Kingdom*. Developed by Lunaris Games and protected by United States and international copyright law. © Lunaris Games. Naja B., "Melanin Friendly Games: 'Errant Kingdom'," *Blerdy Otome* (blog), May 4, 2020, https://blerdyotome.com/2020/05/04/melanin-friendly-games-errant-kingdom/.

of 'Visual Novel': Perfecting Prose.") Narration (in other words, anything that isn't dialogue, including the main character (MC)'s inner thoughts) can have its own text box to differentiate it from dialogue.

Dialogue Text Box

Dialogue text boxes come in two categories: MC dialogue and non-player character (NPC) dialogue. Or the dialogue text box may be the same for both the MC and the NPCs.

If you've played VNs or games that use VN storytelling techniques, you've probably noticed that the speaking character's name appears somewhere on the dialogue textbox (usually on the top left or right, sometimes corresponding with what side of the screen the speaking NPC is on).

CAPTION: Dialogue text box including the speaking character's name (Maja) on the upper-left side of the box. Screenshot from *Errant Kingdom*. Developed by Lunaris Games and protected by United States and international copyright law. © Lunaris Games.
"Errant Kingdom," Lunarisgames.itch.io, accessed May 14, 2022, https://lunarisgames.itch.io/errantkingdom.

The dialogue text box might also include the MC's name. The name can be "You," a name the player chooses, or the fixed-character[1] name of the MC. Or the MC dialogue text box might also have a simpler design, similar to the narrative text box. But it has some characteristic, like color, outlining, etc., that distinguishes it from the narrative and NPC dialogue text boxes.

For more on the nuances of dialogue boxes and their design, please see "Choose Your Words Carefully: Dialogue in Visual Novels and Choice-Based Games."

Choice Text Boxes

Choice text boxes present the dialogue and action choices players can make where the story branches. Like dialogue text boxes, all types of choices can be presented in the same choice text box, or dialogue choices can have a different design than action choices.

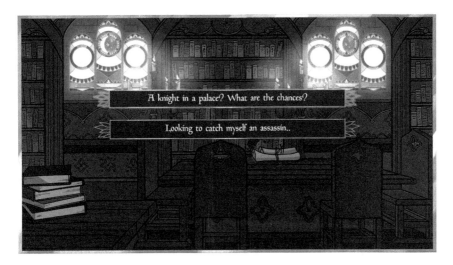

CAPTION: Screenshot from *Errant Kingdom* with dialogue choices. Developed by Lunaris Games and protected by United States and international copyright law. © Lunaris Games. "7269," Tuxdb.com, accessed May 14, 2022, https://tuxdb.com/game/7269.

CHARACTER SPRITES

Character sprites are the visual representations of the MC and NPCs. These sprites can be animated or static images.

Each character in the VN tends to have several emotional states. In other words, the expressions, body language, and postures change to communicate their emotions and reactions to other characters and about situations they find themselves in.

We'll look more at the important roles of character sprites in "Dialogue in Visual Novels and Choice-Based Games: Choose Your Words Carefully" and "Developing Your Own Visual Novels and Choice-Based Games: A Quick Guide."

BACKGROUND ART (ENVIRONMENTAL ART)

The backgrounds represent the world of the VN. They are the locations in which the player and characters navigate. Depending on how large the world is, the VN may have many or only a few backgrounds. The level of detail in the background depends on the VN's aesthetic and the developer's budget. (More detailed art takes longer to produce, which makes it more expensive.) Few details may give players the "suggestion" of what happens at the location, like silhouettes of objects or unadorned buildings. Or the backgrounds can have many details to make the world feel more fleshed out.

CGs

"CG" is short for "computer graphic" but that may not make much sense in relation to visual novels. Simply put, CGs are images, usually illustrations. They may commemorate special moments when unlocked, some things players will discover over the course of their playthroughs. These are images corresponding with an important moment in the story or character route, signaling that players have unlocked content.

Monster Prom's CGs, for example, unlock at the end of a playthrough. If the player successfully woos their choice to ask to prom, they'll get a CG event (read: image) of their player-character in a prom photo with their date. On the flip side, if the player loses and the monster they ask out rejects them, they'll get a CG of the NPC mocking their player-character.

Think of CGs as rewards for reaching an important part of the main story, side story, or another character's story.

You can also use CGs as a form of cutscene. While not animated, a CG's image illustrates an important moment the game wants to emphasize, or it is representative of a scene that suggests action and movement. When used as cutscene images, they usually interrupt the story when they appear on screen to grab the player's attention. These images can be action-based, plot-based, or even character-based. Sometimes these CGs-as-cutscenes are the only thing on the screen, or they can be accompanied by text.

SOUND DESIGN AND SOUNDTRACK

Sounds are an important part of making the world feel inhabited. Sound effects can provide ambient sounds like birdsong, spoons clinking against mugs in cafés, etc. When paired with static backgrounds, these sounds make settings feel dynamic.

Music can also play an important part in the game. Like in other game genres, locations may have their own themes. Giving locations in the world their own soundscape creates a range of atmospheres, from absurdity to horror.

Characters and situations can have their own themes, too. The tone of the themes may reinforce aspects of the characters' personalities. Or, to note a change in the tone of a conversation or circumstance, the VN may use a particular theme. For example, a more serious story may have a theme that signifies a moment of levity or seriousness.

SIMPLE ≠ PLAIN

The assets on the visual novel screen are effective in delivering the game's story, and the ways in which VNs use character sprites, backgrounds, sound, and text boxes are used by other game genres for this reason. Depending on the game's aesthetic, they can be simple or more detailed. "Simple," however, does not mean "plain." Suggesting what a location is like in the world leaves players' imagination to fill in their own details. And when visual assets have sound effects accompanying them, this gives scenes an energy and a sense that the world on the screen is inhabited beyond the characters with which the players are interacting.

NOTE

1 A fixed character has a specific history, personality, and identity. The player does not get to decide any aspects of the fixed character. This is in contrast to cipher characters, customizable characters, or fixed characters with some customization. With these other character types, the player determines some or all of the player-character's look, history, personality, or identity.

CHAPTER 6

The "Novel" Part of "Visual Novel"

Perfecting Prose

Uᴺʟɪᴋᴇ ᴏᴛʜᴇʀ ɢᴀᴍᴇs, ᴠɪsᴜᴀʟ novels (VNs) and some choice-based games use prose writing as a fundamental vehicle for their story-telling. While you do see prose in other games in the form of lore and in menus, in VNs, prose is front and center on the screen. Players interact with it and click on text boxes to advance through the game. Because traditional prose is essential to VNs, there are some prose techniques that can make reading a VN more enjoyable.

PROSE FICTION CONVENTIONS

Most VNs use a basic prose fiction structure; in other words, the writing is in sentences and paragraphs. Players might read through several passages of narration before the game returns to choices

DOI: 10.1201/9781003199724-8

or character interactions. This is similar to novels, where audiences might read a couple of pages of narration before the story returns to action or conversations. Because most VNs have limited art, sound, and animation assets, the prose does the heavy lifting to describe to players what they can't see on the screen or hear or feel via haptic feedback. The prose helps transition from one scene to another, describes what settings are like, gives players a better picture of characters' expressions and reactions, and provides a window into the inner world of the main character (MC). Well-written prose can elevate a good story to a great and memorable one. This doesn't mean that the writing has to be "art" (however one chooses to define that), but it doesn't need to be an afterthought. Players *do* appreciate good prose.

> 04/03/2019
> I don't know about the rest of you but I really loved this chapter. So beautifully written. This is becoming by far one of my favorites on the app.   Do you have any other stories published somewhere? I really like the style of which you write. I would love to read more of your works if they are available.

CAPTION: A player expresses her thoughts with the writer about the prose in a mobile VN.

What techniques can you borrow from prose fiction to write great prose in your VNs?

THE ROLE OF NARRATION

In many ways, the narration is a character, whether it's an "all-seeing eye" that describes the story's action and all of the characters' thoughts to the audience, or whether it's the thoughts, observations, and introspections from a character with a specific point of view. And it can step away from the action to explain how characters are processing their circumstances. The narration should have a strong sense of style and voice. It develops its own identity and is the "authoritative" perspective the audience follows to understand what's happening in the story.

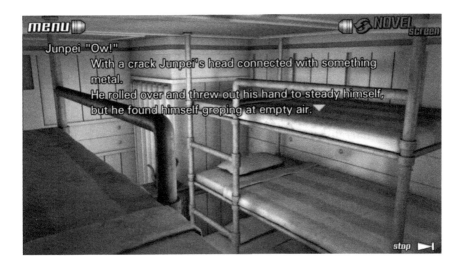

CAPTION: Part of 999's opening scene (PC remaster). The narrator describes the action and what Junpei feels as the player reads and hears the voiced dialogue. Developed by Spike Chunsoft and protected by United States and international copyright law. © Spike Chunsoft, Co. Ltd.
Materwelonz, "Let's Play 999: 9 Hours, 9 Persons, 9 Doors [PC Remaster] Blind Part 1: Zero Escape: Nonary Games," uploaded March 25, 2017, YouTube video, 34:46, https://www.youtube.com/watch?v=LE3djgiH2XU&list=PLAIcZs9N4173 EEQMkwJOnszpx_2B0QZH_.

The Role of Character-As-Narrator

The MC's narrative voice fosters a connection between them and the player. It represents the MC's inner monologues, observations about the action the player's experiencing, the MC's true thoughts about other characters, and the MC's perspective of and outlook on the world. Their narration builds the emotional connection between player and MC, and influences how the player views other characters. Just as the MC should have a distinctive style and voice in their dialogue, they should also have a distinctive style in their narration.

The Unreliable Narrator

The unreliable narrator is a fixture in fiction, and this includes VNs. To some degree, *every* point-of-view character is unreliable because they often don't have all of the facts, they're swayed by their opinions of others, and they have prejudices and biases that cloud their perceptions. They will always lack some credibility for these reasons. But unreliable narrators, who usually narrate in first-person point of view ("I/me/my"), intentionally mislead their audience or are misleading because their perception of reality is so skewed. Some unreliable narrators make sense because they're the actual villain, they're hiding their guilt (not necessarily over a crime or injustice done to someone else), or they're otherwise impaired in a way that they can't see reality clearly. Another type of unreliable narrator is *not* the MC or protagonist, but other characters who detail events to the MC, hiding the truth for a myriad of reasons, basing reality on their prejudices, or lacking the ability to remember accurately and treating their faulty memories as truth. (Witnesses in the *Ace Attorney* series are good examples of this.) This type of character should seem less and less trustworthy as the game goes on. This means you will have to carefully breadcrumb clues about their unreliability, as "an unreliable narrator's version of events and characters in the story will also build to reveal, simultaneously, his/her own personal prejudices, anxieties, fears, tastes, delusions, and even beliefs."[1]

SCENE SETTING AND ATMOSPHERE

VNs generally do not have 3D environments that are explorable, being limited to static two-dimensional backgrounds that represent the game world's locations. The narration, then, describes to the player what they can and can't see. The three-dimensionality comes through the prose itself. The background might be of the outside of a museum with a fountain. There are no people or animals in the drawing. The prose assists players in imagining that this is a lively public space with lots of tourists, locals taking leisurely walks with their dogs, and pigeons splashing in the fountain. Players can hear without sound assets as the narrator talks about the cooing pigeons flapping their wings in the fountain water. They can listen in on the conversations and hear people laughing.

But the narrator's scene setting goes beyond describing the location. Establishing sense of place also incorporates the tension/conflict and emotion, the atmosphere (feeling or mood) players sense from the scene and narrative.

The duffel bag unzips violently in the quiet night as Ryan opens it.

CAPTION: *Siren Song* screenshots from the Moments app. Developed by STARDUST and protected by United States and international copyright law. © STARDUST.

(*Continued*)

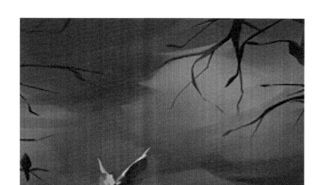

He hands his mother a gigantic axe.

CAPTION (*Continued*): *Siren Song* screenshots from the Moments app. Developed by STARDUST and protected by United States and international copyright law. © STARDUST.

(*Continued*)

I press my face against the cold crypt as
the axe swings down.

CAPTION (*Continued*): *Siren Song* screenshots from the Moments app. Developed by STARDUST and protected by United States and international copyright law. © STARDUST.

Siren Song has a graveyard scene where one of Cecilia's friends is executed after being caught by monster hunters. Using only tombstones and a statue as the backdrop, I had to convey the MC's horror as the action unfolds, and she's unable to stop her friend from being killed. The mood is somber and the atmosphere tense. Cecilia narrates to the player what she sees, feels, and hears, and expresses her sense of hopelessness.

CHARACTERIZATION

Similar to the narration describing places in the world, it also illustrates fuller pictures of characters than art can convey. Beyond telling players about appearances, the narrator can also explain characters' demeanors, the vibes or energy they give off, the way they make the MC feel in positive and negative ways, and other bits of characterization that help players get a better sense of who characters are.

It's impossible to overlook her. What with the way she towers over us!

CAPTION: *The Letter* screenshots. Developed by Yangyang Mobile and protected by United States and international copyright law. © Yangyang Mobile.

(*Continued*)

CAPTION (*Continued*): *The Letter* screenshots. Developed by Yangyang Mobile and protected by United States and international copyright law. © Yangyang Mobile.

ManlyBadassHero, "*The Letter*: Hey … Pass It On (Ch.1) Manly Let's Play [2]," uploaded July 26, 2017, YouTube video, 52:08, https://www.youtube.com/watch?v=qSzo7jzaBlM&list=PLq7Wze90TsOob5eW_3Cm6qLbK2YKlh1KU&index=2.

In this scene from *The Letter* (2017), Isabella describes Marianne (on the left) upon meeting her. Marianne strikes an imposing figure, and she intimidates Isabella. None of this is obvious from Marianne's sprite, nor can we see Isabella's reactions to Marianne. We rely on Isabella's narration for a more nuanced characterization of Marianne.

EXPOSITION IN VISUAL NOVELS

Exposition is a literary device that gives the audience necessary background information about the world and its settings, history, characters, and even plot. It often "sets the stage" at the beginning of the story. These expository passages introduce the audience to relevant information that "catches them up to speed" about what's currently happening in the world and how the characters they meet are involved.

Opening with exposition is a convention in VNs because it helps to ground players in the world. However, opening with long narrative passages may not be the best way to begin the story. Yes, players expect to read in VNs, but some passages can be too-long infodumps (a large amount of information piled onto the audience at once), and forcing them to read a lot can potentially bore the player. At the start of the game, players may want to get right into the action. The longer the expository narration goes on, the more anxious or irritated the player becomes.

Some exposition is usually necessary. Consider where the best place is to present it. Is it at the beginning, or do you open in a scene, and then step back from the action for a little exposition? How do you get into the story quickly? Do you sprinkle bits of exposition throughout the main story and some branches? Is some information better shared through dialogue instead of narration?

SENSORY DETAILS, SUBTEXT, AND ENGAGING THE PLAYER'S IMAGINATION

Narration can set the scene, provide characterization, be a connection between MC and player, and introduce lore, but it can still be "just okay" prose. There's one simple technique writers can use to make the prose emotionally poignant. This literary device, sensory detail, actively works to place players in the scene and engage their imaginations.

Characteristics of "Okay" Writing

Through reading and editing—no matter the medium—over the past couple of years, I was finding a lot of prose to be good, not great. I was wondering, "What's going on? There are good ideas here, but it's not as satisfying as it could be." Then I realized everything was surface level with no **subtext**. When prose has no subtext, everything is "on the surface." "Subtext" literally means "under or beneath (sub-) the text." Stories have literal meanings. There are the actual words the audience reads. However, stories can also have hidden meanings—emotional, metaphorical, and thematic takeaways that are not explicitly narrated. These hidden meanings make up the subtext, that which is below the literal text. The text is to the conscious as the subtext is to the subconscious.

On-the-surface writing lacks the nuance of subtext. It tells the audience how to feel. It's on the nose in explaining character motivations and expressing their emotions. While it may still engage the reader's imagination, it doesn't provide any metaphorical or thematic content that connects the reader to deeper, more emotionally resonant meanings in the story. On-the-surface writing tells and doesn't show. But it also lacks other strengths of writing with subtext.

CHARACTERISTICS OF SURFACE-LEVEL WRITING

- Lacks descriptive writing
- Lacks sensory details
- Tells readers/players everything
- Doesn't encourage readers/players to use their imaginations
- Is not as engaging as it could be

When I was reading a lot of "decent but not great prose," I realized something that it lacked was sensory details.

Sensory details are descriptive writing that evokes the five senses. They show and don't tell because they allow the audience to enter the scene and hear, see, touch, taste, and smell everything that's happening for themselves. This is *literally* effective because reading sensory descriptions activates the sensory cortex in the brain and immerses the reader in the scene.[2] If a character touches a hot stove and shrieks, you don't have to explain that she's in pain. When characters walk into a room and they're hit with something putrid and they gag, you don't have to tell your audience that they're repulsed. Adding sensory details was one of the techniques I learned in workshops as a young writer who never imagined she'd be working on games someday, and it's a common suggestion I make when I'm editing games and other storytelling media. This might be a review for some of you, but discussing old techniques we've learned is never a bad thing.

Surface vs. Subtext

Scene One	Scene Two
Alice yelled at Mark as soon as he walked through the front door. "Where have you been?!" Mark feared his wife would be even more angry if he told her, so he retreated to the bedroom.	Alice's voice thundered down the hallway as soon as Mark slinked through the door. "Where have you been?!" His cheeks reddened. He bowed his head and tiptoed to the bedroom.

CAPTION: Image made in Google Slides. © Toiya Kristen Finley.

"Scene One" and "Scene Two" both involve the same incident with the same characters. In "Scene One," there's some subtext. Alice yells. Clearly, she's angry. The reader can imagine the sound of her voice, its intensity, and how loud it is. But then the narration *tells* you how Mark's feeling and explains his motives. He's afraid of telling his wife where he was. So, to avoid her, he goes to their bedroom. "Scene One" is mostly surface-level writing. In "Scene Two," Alice's voice thunders. You're not told that she's yelling—you can hear it. Thundering is also intimidating, and you can see this as Mark slinks into the house. In slinking, he's making himself small, which also hints at the shame he is feeling. Mark's cheeks redden, signifying that he's embarrassed. He bows his head, also symbolic of his shame. Unlike in "Scene One," "Scene Two" doesn't tell us that Mark retreats to the bedroom—it describes him retreating and the manner in which he does it. The fact that he tiptoes also suggests that he doesn't want Alice to know where he is. "Scene Two's" subtext gives you a better feel for these characters' behaviors, their personalities, and their history together. All of "Scene Two's" subtext comes through sensory details.

Take a moment to read both scenes again. Focus on the differences. Point out the sensory details and descriptions in the scenes and note how these techniques help (or don't help) you visualize what's happening.

Invite Players to Use Their Imaginations

One thing to keep in mind is that players' imaginations are powerful storytelling tools. I would say they are the most powerful—and most important—tools. Games are successful whether they have photorealistic or retro graphics. They're successful experiences when their stories are 80-hours long and there are lots of non-player characters (NPCs) to interact with, or the game takes less than half an hour to play, and there's nothing but text on the screen.

So, we don't have to show or tell players everything for them to find the narrative enjoyable.

Sensory details work so well because they play upon our own, real sensory experiences in how we've interacted with our physical world. They activate our imaginations. If we read, "The bread crumbled in his mouth as he bit into it," we all know what it feels like to bite into and eat bread. This shared experience builds empathy with the character. We might even feel the bread in our mouths.

This writer had an … interesting experience eating a sausage sandwich from Burger King[3]:

> I love Sausage McMuffins and went for Burger King's knock off. Imagine an English muffin soaked in artificial butter oil, toasted, assembled with a spongy egg-like substance, cheese whiz or something, and a sausage puck. Now, wait a few hours, microwave until completely indestructible, and serve to an unsuspecting consumer. It was malevolently bad.

This is from someone's Facebook post. Nowhere does it say, "This is what the sandwich tasted like and what it felt like in my mouth." In the case of the Burger King Sausage McMuffin knockoff, what tastes and feels bad to you may not taste and feel bad to me. If you're a vegetarian and you can't stand meat, your reaction to this passage may be a little more visceral than the meat eaters reading this. But if you had any reaction at all on the spectrum of "yuck!," you were immersed in the retelling of this experience. Your imagination was engaged, and you may have been empathizing with the writer as you read the passage. Go back and analyze the taste, sight, and touch details in the writing. What are they, and how do you react to them?

When we use sensory details, we're encouraging the audience to be a part of the experience they're reading and to actively imagine it.

Sensory Details in Interactive Stories

This means sensory details are great for interactive stories and VNs, and we have many opportunities to use them. Their inclusion is actually an advantage that text-based games have over other types of games. While players may be able to explore 2D or 3D environments and hear sounds, descriptive texts can illustrate the mood of the environment or a conversation between characters. Text can characterize sounds as menacing or goofy. Text can give players a sense of what things taste and feel like. The extent of what players can feel is through haptic feedback and how easy or difficult it is to maneuver vehicles, machinery, weapons, and other objects via controls.

Except for a recent experiment,[4] tasting is something players can't do in games. Descriptive writing and sensory details can create specific atmospheric, thematic, and subtextual information that rely on players' imaginations. Not relying on their imaginations is akin to the monster being scarier in a film or show before it's revealed onscreen because our minds know what's scary to *us* individually. The monster that ends up onscreen is what someone *else* thinks is scary. Sometimes, it's better for players to have their own picture they're visualizing in their minds, instead of a physical embodiment on a screen.

Sensory details place players in the scene through descriptive writing.

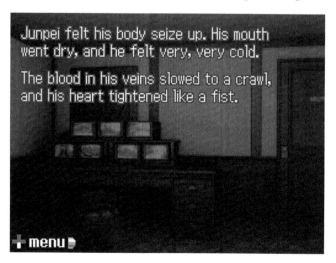

CAPTION: Touch details in a passage from *999*. Developed by Spike Chunsoft and protected by United States and international copyright law. © Spike Chunsoft, Co. Ltd. Dragonatrix, "*999: Nine Hours, Nine Persons, Nine Doors* Part 42: Hallway 7," Let's Play Archive, accessed May 15, 2022, https://lparchive.org/999-Nine-Hours-Nine-Persons-Nine-Doors/Update42/.

In this scene from 999, there's no art corresponding with what Junpei is experiencing. We don't see Junpei's sprite. We aren't even inside his head, privy to his thoughts. However, what's described brings players into an intimate moment where Junpei and other characters find a dead body, and what Junpei sees is so horrible, so sickening and visceral, that his body is responding traumatically. It's physically uncomfortable. The mood is one of terror and dread. We can encourage players to experience what the characters are experiencing and to empathize with them. Sensory details are especially helpful in this way if you have limited art and sound assets, or if you don't have any at all. One reason great prose in VNs is elevated is due to sensory details like the ones in this scene from 999.

FUNCTIONS OF SENSORY DETAILS

- Build the scene through descriptive writing
- Put the player in the scene
- Enhance the scene whether you have art/sound assets or not

Sensory Details Engage the Player's Imagination

When we add sensory details, we're making players active participants beyond choosing paths and dialogue choices and reading until the next choice. Because sensory details add subtext, you don't have to explain or state the obvious. Writers have heard the maxim "Show, don't tell" ad nauseam, and I've referenced it in this chapter. But, sometimes, "show" can be on the nose and ineffective, just like telling. For example:

"The bells made an awful sound."

Players know what bells sound like, and they can sense how bells can be cacophonous and unappealing. However, this description *tells* the player the sound is awful. It doesn't illustrate an awful sound.

"The bells clanged" is more meaningful and impactful than "The bells made an awful sound."

Sensory details allow players to infer and interpret what they're reading, which makes it more real to them because they're drawing their own meanings out of the story. And, if you're working with word limitations (and even if you're not), you can use fewer words with them: "clanged" vs. "made an awful sound."

Beyond Sight: All Five Senses

One thing I've noticed about prose in fiction, nonfiction, and in games is that writers tend to describe what things look like or what a character sees, and we don't focus as much on the other senses.

But they're *all* important:

Sight: "… slinked through the door."

Touch: "… his heart tightened like a fist."

Smell: "Salt sweeping across the ocean air stung his nostrils."

Sound: "… thundered down the hallway …"

Taste: "… English muffin soaked in artificial butter oil …"

Note how none of these are obvious—they don't tell the reader how they should feel or respond to the sensory information. The writer isn't eating the English muffin, only describing how it's soaked in artificial butter oil. This *implies* that it has the overwhelming taste of artificial butter and that it's too oily (touch). It doesn't say that the character smells the salt, but the description evokes the smell of sea salt and that it's powerful and piercing in his nose.

BEYOND ADJECTIVES AND NOUNS: SENSORY PARTS OF SPEECH

Something else to keep in mind is that verbs and dreaded adverbs[5] are just as descriptive and sensory as nouns and adjectives. So, be thoughtful with your word choice.

Looking again at the example from *999*, we get how Junpei feels through verbs as well as adjectives:

"His mouth went **dry**, and he felt very, very **cold**."

"The blood in his veins **slowed** to a crawl."

"… his heart **tightened** like a fist."

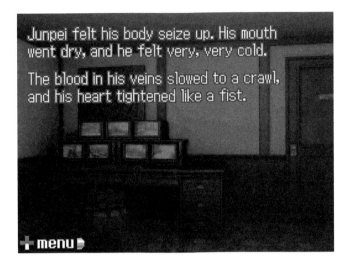

CAPTION: The verbs "tightened" and "slowed" and the adjectives "dry" and "cold" evoke touch. Developed by Spike Chunsoft and protected by United States and international copyright law. © Spike Chunsoft, Co. Ltd.
Dragonatrix, "999: Nine Hours, Nine Persons, Nine Doors Part 42: Hallway 7," Let's Play Archive, accessed May 15, 2022, https://lparchive.org/999-Nine-Hours-Nine-Persons-Nine-Doors/Update42/.

We learn that adjectives are descriptors that modify nouns. Verbs describe what someone or something is doing and how they do it. Adverbs themselves are descriptors because they modify verbs and adjectives. Other parts of speech are effective descriptors in the way that they characterize or give attributes to other words in a sentence or phrase.

Back to that scene I referenced from *Siren Song* earlier in the chapter … I had been thinking a lot about sensory details when I wrote *Siren Song*, a visual novel for mobile. I wanted to make sure I put what I was thinking about into practice. In this scene, I use verbs and adverbs. (And these screenshots are a few paragraphs apart.)

The duffel bag unzips violently in the quiet night as Ryan opens it.

CAPTION: Screenshot from *Siren Song*. Developed by STARDUST and protected by United States and international copyright law. © STARDUST.

"The duffel bag **unzips violently** in the **quiet** night …"

I could have used "unzips with a violence" or "unzips with violence," but that's wordier, it slows down the action, and doesn't seem as, well, violent as a result.

THE IMPORTANCE OF WORD CHOICE

And just to reiterate the importance of word choice, words influence the impressions you give the reader/player and develop your subtext. It's good to be more thoughtful about the best words to use during your revision process.

One word can change your perspective:

If you read "She clomped up the stairs," how old do you think she is?

"The bells rang"

is a different sound than

"the bells chimed,"

which is a different sound than

"the bells clanged."

HOW LONG IS TOO LONG?

Exposition can get too long, but so can any narrative passages, no matter how well they're written. While players expect to read, they do reach a limit where they can get exhausted or bored.

How long is too long is relative, but you might consider what's comfortable to read. In an age of reading on smartphone screens, people are becoming more and more used to reading shorter paragraphs. Also, the longer a paragraph or passage is, the more difficult it is to retain information. Quality assurance (QA) or game testers can help identify passages that are too long. If you have a small team or you're the only one making the game, you can ask friends or any supporters you might have to note where they feel their interest starts to wane or they get a sense of "Get on with it!"

Some mobile VN studios have strict writing guidelines where paragraphs can be only so many lines or characters (letters, punctuation, and spaces—not just words). If you're not working on a mobile VN, you can always approximate their minimum and maximum lengths as a standard for your own narration.

A final note on sensory details and descriptive writing in general: Don't go overboard, unless the style of the prose is intentionally purple.[6] Too many descriptors can slow down the action or bog down the writing by making it overly complicated. It can be a slog to read.

KEYS TO EFFECTIVE PROSE

The VN's narrator builds an emotional connection between the player and the story. Often the MC or player-character, the narrator gives players a window into their inner worlds and how they're observing and processing everything going on around them. The voice of the narrator, combined with thoughtful descriptive writing and subtextual meanings, has the ability to involve the reader in the action.

Sensory details further invite players into a more personal reading experience by engaging their imaginations, especially if you have limited assets. How players imagine sensory details will be unique to them.

Use *all* of the five senses.

And, remember, verbs and adverbs are sensory, too!

EXERCISES

1. Establishing the Narrator

    Write a short narrative passage that sets the scene at a location. The narrator does not have to be the main character.

2. Sensory Detail Revision

    Now, go back and add sensory detail to your narrative passage. If you already have these details, think about whether you could be more accurate: "she laughed" vs. "she giggled and snorted."

    • Do the sensory details and other descriptive writing establish a subtext in the scene? What does the subtext evoke?

If you already have narrative passages in your portfolio or past work, consider reviewing them and adding sensory details and/or other descriptive language.

NOTES

1 Neil Davison, "What Is an Unreliable Narrator?" Oregon State Guide to Literary Terms, accessed May 2, 2022, https://liberalarts.oregonstate.edu/wlf/what-unreliable-narrator.

2 Annie Murphy Paul, "Your Brain on Fiction," *The New York Times*, March 17, 2012, http://www.nytimes.com/2012/03/18/opinion/sunday/the-neuro-science-of-your-brain-on-fiction.html.

3 Kim Kautzer, "Describing a Food: The Good, the Bad, and the Ugly," WriteShop, July 30, 2018, https://writeshop.com/describing-a-food-the-good-the-bad-and-the-ugly/.

4 Hope Corrigan, "A Lickable Screen That Can Imitate Flavours Is in Development," PC Gamer, December 30, 2021, https://www.pcgamer.com/a-lickable-screen-that-can-imitate-flavours-is-in-development/.

5 Some writing advice declares you should not use adverbs, or use them sparingly. (Whoops … Guess that's my quota for adverbs in this footnote.)

6 Overly ornate and poetic writing. If there's a good reason for using purple prose (highlighting the pretentiousness of a character, parodying a certain style or genre), try doling it out in small doses.

CHAPTER 7

Designing Branching Narratives

Choices, Variables, and Relationships

E XCEPT FOR KINETIC VISUAL novels (VNs) with linear plots, visual novels are known for their branching narratives and multiple endings. The process of journeying through the variety of a story's plot arcs and getting to those endings is part of what makes VNs and other choice-based games so satisfying for players.

Designing that branching is an important undertaking for both narrative designers and writers on the project, and it can be an intimidating task, even for veterans who've worked on several interactive titles. What is the main story (critical path)? Where will points in the main story diverge? How many non-player characters (NPCs) will get their own routes? Are there variables that determine what story content the player experiences? How many endings should there be? While you can be ambitious with how the story might change with each choice and variable, you want the branching to remain *manageable*. It's very easy for branching to get unwieldy if you don't have a plan before you start writing and designing the story. If you're writing for a client, they'll probably give you a few parameters like the number of total chapters, how many choices per chapter, etc. So, when you're given some structure, staying in control of the branching design is easier. When you're writing your own story or if you don't have parameters or a template in place, there are several aspects of your story's design that you'll have to consider. As we discuss plotting branching narrative, we'll work to demystify this process.

BRANCHING NARRATIVE STRUCTURES

Not only does the complexity of your branching structure affect the story experience, but it also can be quite costly. More branching means longer production times, more assets to create, and more budget. Think of BioWare's triple-A franchises, *Mass Effect* and *Dragon Age*. Certain choices open up the world to new levels and characters. That means there are thousands of assets that have to be developed per choice. There are strategies you can use to get around needing a massive budget to release a longer, more complex story. But keep the axiom of "good, fast, or cheap" in mind. You can have two of three, but not all three. Without a large budget, the world you create may have to be smaller with fewer locations and characters, you may have to reuse assets, your team might be small, and it might take you a long time to finish your project.

You don't, however, need a triple-A budget to design a great story. In fact, players support indie VNs because they love the stories and characters. So, how do you begin to approach plotting your story, where it branches, and what choices you'll give players? Let's review some types of branching structures that you might use.

Branching Structures with Fewer Endings

Some structures can be mostly linear, except for a few choices that can determine aspects of the story, like actions the main character (MC) takes to move the plot along, actions or dialogue the player chooses that can affect how NPCs feel or view the MC, and one or a few endings. If the story has one ending, the different relationship choices and routes along the way can make playthroughs feel different from one another. For example, at the end of the story, you finally find the treasure you've been searching for. In one playthrough, you steal your best friend's map and then proceed to the treasure's location. In another playthrough, your friend says you can split the loot, and you find the treasure together. You always end up with the treasure at the end, but you may or may not still have a best friend.

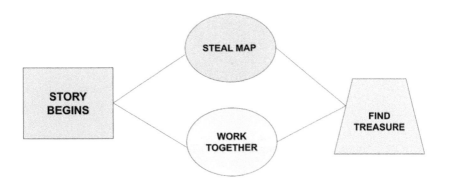

CAPTION: Image made in Google Slides. © Toiya Kristen Finley.

Whether or not you still have a best friend is a **variable**. To put it simply, a variable is a stored bit of information that the game tracks. The game will track certain variables based on the player's gameplay and choices. So, stealing the map is one variable (not best friends) and working together is another (are best friends). Based on this example, the game checks for whether the player still has a best friend when reaching the ending and gives the player the appropriate scenario at the end of the game (*split the loot with your best friend* or *find the treasure alone and friendless*).

Now, this is a *very* simple branching structure, but variables can give you different outcomes, even if the branching is simple. Simple structures can have a bit more complexity with added branches.

A structure can have one or two endings, but there may be branching off of branches, or **nested branches**. In other words, a choice can lead to a section of the story with more choices before that section rejoins or remerges with the main plot.

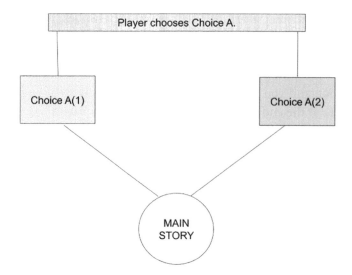

CAPTION: Image made in Google Slides. © Toiya Kristen Finley.

Paul Nelson refers to this as a "*foldback structure,* where the player has choices, but these branches eventually all lead to the same place."[1]

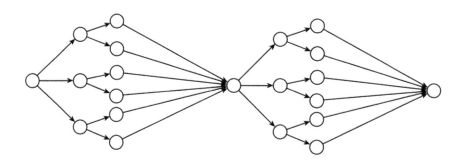

CAPTION: Paul Nelson, "Designing Branching Narrative," *The Story Element* (blog), February 11, 2015, https://thestoryelement.wordpress.com/2015/02/11/designing-branching-narrative/.

As Nelson notes, the danger in the foldback structure is that it can make players feel their choices are meaningless because all branches "eventually lead to the same conclusion."[2] However, the player's experience *can* feel meaningful with variables and changes in relationships with various characters—and these the player can most definitely control. In fact, there are VNs where there is only one LI and one or two endings. The player's decisions can determine whether the MC and LI live happily ever after, or not.

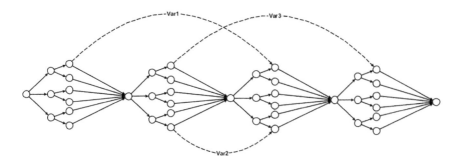

CAPTION: Paul Nelson, "Designing Branching Narrative," *The Story Element* (blog), February 11, 2015, https://thestoryelement.wordpress.com/2015/02/11/designing-branching-narrative/.

In the diagram, variables are labeled "Var1," "Var2," and "Var3." Var1 leads to the third nested branch, bypassing the second nested branch, which the player will not experience on that playthrough. Var2 leads from the second nested branch into the third, so the player would experience the second, third, and last nested branch. Var3 leads from the second nested branch to the last. So, while there is only one ending, the three variables dictate different playthroughs and story experiences.[3]

If you're planning for player-character deaths or "game overs" when players make certain choices, a gauntlet structure makes sense. Gauntlets have a more linear story structure, and they branch off into failed endings and deaths.

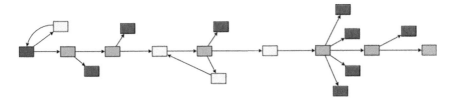

CAPTION: Sam Kabo Ashwell, "Standard Patterns in Choice-Based Games," *These Heterogenous Tasks* (blog), January 26, 2015, https://heterogenoustasks.wordpress.com/2015/01/26/standard-patterns-in-choice-based-games/.

A gauntlet structure also allows the player a little freedom to explore branches and return to previous choices in the story to try other routes.[4]

These structures, while only having one or two endings or "game overs," can have lots of variations, as illustrated above. They can also be used to structure subplots within the overall story or character routes. Sam and Mike's fates in *Until Dawn* (Supermassive Games, 2015) are great examples of this. Throughout the game, the other seven main characters have several ways they can die. They may or may not make it to the end for the final confrontation with the wendigos. However, Sam and Mike, no matter what choices players make or quick-time events they miss playing as them, always make it to that last scene. Whether they live or die is determined in the final moments of the game. That does not, however, mean that Sam and Mike don't face hardships or injury. (Mike can lose a finger based on player decision-making, for example.)

More Complex Branching

With a complex narrative, not only might it have multiple endings, but it might also have multiple nested branches branching off of other multiple nested branches to get to some endings. Conclusions to the story can be wildly different from one another. What Sam Kabo Ashwell calls the **time cave** is one structure that can lead to multiple endings that are seemingly detached from each other, almost as if they're stories from similar yet different dimensions than the original story because the branches never rejoin a main story. Classic *Choose Your Own Adventure* novels follow this structure, as well.[5]

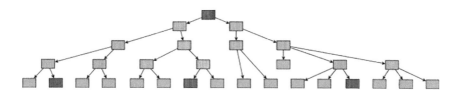

CAPTION: Sam Kabo Ashwell, "Standard Patterns in Choice-Based Games," *These Heterogenous Tasks* (blog), January 26, 2015, https://heterogenoustasks. wordpress.com/2015/01/26/standard-patterns-in-choice-based-games/.

Time caves result in short playthroughs and encourage replayability because of the possibilities of wildly divergent endings.[6] If you're looking to give players shorter, more surreal experiences, the time cave structure may be appealing.

A branching structure that does rejoin the main story is the **branch and bottleneck**. It has multiple endings and nested branching. It also makes use of variables to determine which parts of the branching structure the player experiences: "the branches regularly rejoin, usually around events that are common to all versions of the story."[7]

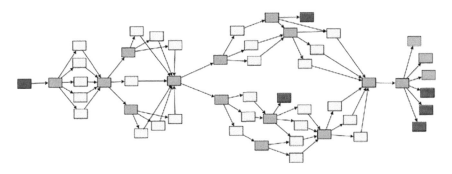

CAPTION: Sam Kabo Ashwell, "Standard Patterns in Choice-Based Games," *These Heterogenous Tasks* (blog), January 26, 2015, https://heterogenoustasks. wordpress.com/2015/01/26/standard-patterns-in-choice-based-games/.

Complex branching can become unwieldy if it's not carefully plotted, and that plotting includes being mindful of what happens in each plot point and story beat and tracking variables.[8] You can accidentally introduce plot holes or other story inconsistencies. To see just what kind of branching and variable tracking you might be responsible for, here is *Black Mirror: Bandersnatch*'s flowchart.

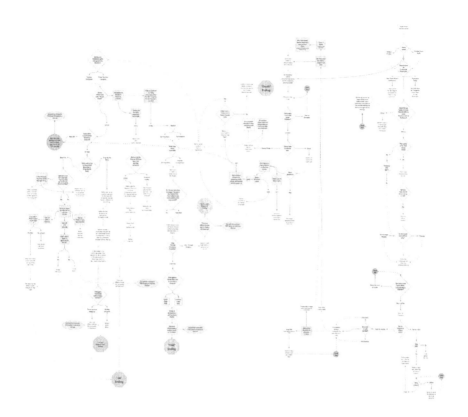

CAPTION: Various contributors. "*Bandersnatch* Map: All Choices and Outcomes," IGN, last modified January 10, 2019, https://www.ign.com/wikis/black-mirror/Bandersnatch_Map_-_All_Choices_and_Outcomes.

Branch Lengths

How long should each branch be before it rejoins the main story or leads to an ending? Branches can be all different lengths. They can have their own substantial subplots, or they can be side quests. They can also be Easter eggs, rewards for the player's exploration and trying different choices, or short conversations and scenes that give players new insights into NPCs. Branches that are a part of the plot will probably be longer, while side quests and Easter eggs can feel like fun diversions. Sam Maggs, who has worked on BioWare titles, defines a well-designed branch as "a separate story that makes equal amount of sense" with all of the other branches.[9]

Whatever their lengths, they should feel balanced and have some meaning for existing, Christian Divine (lead writer for *Life Is Strange*, *The Awesome Adventures of Captain Spirit*, and *Life Is Strange 2*) suggests, even if they're humorous or lead to a joke.[10]

Back to the finding treasure example and whether or not the player-character screws over their friend ... Let's look at how the branches could be *un*balanced.

STEAL MAP	WORK TOGETHER
1. Player steals best friend's map from best friend's hotel room.	1. Player and best friend agree to share loot when they find the treasure.
2. Player takes a flight to the island on the map.	2. They leave for the island on the map.
3. Player enters cave on the island and finds a strange puzzle.	3. They enter cave on the island and find a strange puzzle.
4. Player figures out puzzle to reveal the treasure.	4. Player figures out puzzle to reveal the treasure.
5. Player jets away to a remote paradise, so their former best friend can't find them.	5. Sentient rock guardians protecting the treasure attack the player and best friend.
	6. Player and best friend fend off the guardians and escape the cave.
	7. Player and best friend jet away to a remote paradise.

CAPTION: Image made in Google Slides. © Toiya Kristen Finley.

The "Work Together" branch has seven plot points to the "Steal Map" branch's five. "Work Together" is also more of an exciting adventure. The player has more to do and has enemies to fight. While "Steal Map" also has the puzzle to solve, it's not as interesting. There's more *story* to "Work Together." The danger in unbalanced branches is what TV Tropes[11] calls "story branch favoritism": "a particular branch of the story features more content, is better developed than others, and/or dovetails better with the plot overall."[12]

To make branches more balanced, give them and their sub-branches within the nesting the same number of plot points and story beats. If they *don't* have the same number, they at least need to have similar *consequential* outcomes. Divine puts it this way: "... even with branching, follow one story to its end ... I put equal weight into every single branch." He defines "weight" as "emotional weight" and "character weight."[13]

DESIGNING AND PLOTTING

You may need to share your branching design with a team or visualize it for yourself. There are all sorts of ways you can do this. Naturally, if your client or employer has a specific technique for documenting this, you want to follow it.

Otherwise, do this in the best way that makes sense to you and to whomever you'll need to communicate your planning. This can be through a flowchart, linear outline in a Word or Google doc, a prototype in Twine or ink, or even sticky notes arranged on a wall or whiteboard. How best can everyone *visualize* and *keep track* of the main plot, plot arcs and character arcs, and the paths leading to all endings?

Some Questions to Ask While Designing the Main Story and Its Branches

What Does the Player Need to Experience/See? These are the story's main plot points. Players need to experience them to understand the story and progress through the game. If the story has a lot of complex branching like in the time cave or branch and bottleneck, then each branch may have its own main plot points.

Where Will the Branches Diverge from the Main Plot? If there's a main story and the game doesn't branch into a bunch of diverse plots, you'll need to figure out timing. How long should players have in between choices? How long will a branch be before it rejoins the main branch/story? Data suggest the industry standard is about "20–30 minutes of play" between branches.[14] (Mobile, where players don't expect to spend that much time in an app, doesn't apply here.) It might come down to playtesting to get this right, but trying to balance branches can help.

What Will Be Major Choices? Major choices are great places for branches to diverge because they have the ability to alter the story and cause conflict for the player, potentially changing relationships with NPCs and leading to later consequences like deciding the fate of relationships or even NPC or MC deaths.

Once you've formulated or have been given your high-level summaries and/or questions, it can help to list all of the scenes that will (or will potentially) be in the game and in what sections or branches they will appear. If breaking down scenes in this way isn't part of your process, you might break down the story into arcs, major plot points, or major story beats. Note where players will be learning key information, where they fill face conflict, where their relationships have the ability to change for better or worse, and where they could be making choices.

MOBILE VNS AND BRANCHING NARRATIVE

One reason why developers find VNs so attractive to release on mobile is because they don't require a lot of art, animation, sound, or music assets. Mobile's technological and storage limitations are strengths when it comes to VNs. For this reason, mobile VNs don't require a lot of complex branching and multiple endings. Cass Phillips, the Director of Story at Episode (Pocket Gems, Inc.), notes that analytical data prove players are more engaged by relationships and how their choices affect characters' lives, not the main plot.[15]

While you can have lots of branching and multiple endings (I wrote a mobile VN with seven endings!), that's not necessarily an expectation of mobile. You can focus on designing a story with one or two endings with the majority of the choices influencing and changing the MC's relationships and allowing the player to express what they want the MC's personality to be.

KEEPING TRACK OF VARIABLES AND BRANCHING

Since variables are stored data, they can be just about any type of information. These are some common variables in choice-based games:

- **Skills and Skill Levels:** Players acquire skills, and they can increase and decrease them. The game will check to see if players have the right skills and/or skill level in order to unlock content, like a dialogue option or weapon. If players don't have that skill, or the skill level isn't high enough, the check will act as a gate.[16]

- **Abilities or Traits:** Similar to skills, abilities or traits allow players to solve puzzles, defeat enemies, engage NPCs, interact with the environment, etc., by using the ability or trait.

- **Items Acquired:** Players might find items in the environment. They can use the items in puzzles, give them to NPCs, etc. Sometimes, giving NPCs the right item can improve their relationships, lead to romance, or even unlock plot-based branches.

- **Other Stats:** How much of the in-game currency the player has, what they're wearing, whom they've befriended or antagonized, what jobs they work, etc., can unlock parts of the story.

Even if your game only has one or a couple of variables, you'll still need to keep track of them, where they unlock or gate content, and how they influence what the player sees and what endings they get.

Keep a List of Your Variables: If you're using a scripting language like ink, you can create this list directly in your project file. Make sure to keep the list updated. At different points during the development process, you might be adding variables.

Give Variables Easy-to-Understand and Identifiable Names: At a glance, the name of the variable tells you exactly what it is. Names like "Ability1," "Ability2," and "Ability3" are too general, and you'll constantly be looking back at documentation to refresh your memory as to whether *Smooth Operator* is Ability1 or Ability2. Names like "SmoothOperator," "ArmTwister," and "ToughNegotiator" immediately tell you what they are.

Add Variables to Your Outline, Diagram, or Flowchart: Write down where players acquire variables and where those variables will unlock conditional branches,[17] scenes, action and dialogue choices, endings, and/or influence relationships. It may help to color code variables by giving each one a unique color (if you don't have a lot) or color code them by type.

Whatever textual and visual language you're using to track variables, make sure that everyone who has to work with these documents can understand them. Remember that game development documentation is living, meaning that it can be revised and updated. Game docs are *expected* to be updated with several versions. You might seek feedback from your team on how to best tweak and refine your branching structure documentation and outlines until it is easily accessible for everyone. The first draft doesn't have to be perfect.

DESIGNING MULTIPLE ENDINGS

Unlocking endings is one of the more enjoyable aspects of playing choice-based games. Whether players are attempting to get a certain ending on their fifth playthrough, or they're playing the game for the first time without metagaming, that ending they do get is a reward for making it through the entire game and going on journeys with several NPCs. Endings are just as important as plot arcs or character development. There are several issues to consider when designing them so that these endings are satisfying. As with everything else in game development, your budget is going to be a determining factor in how many endings you will have. Separate endings need their own assets. You may have special tracks that play only in the endings. You might need additional character art because characters' clothing, expressions, or other things about them have changed. The endings may take place in areas of the world the player has never seen. And multiple endings mean more production time.

Let's say you have the budget and time for several endings. A very first important question: Does the game *need* multiple endings? As already discussed, one ending can have slight variations. Multiple endings for the sake of multiple endings may not serve the story because that can "result in a lot of writing that feels forced and unnecessary."[18] There are good reasons to have multiple endings: choices of significance lead to several final outcomes, or endings are based on the MC's relationships with several NPCs, including romance stories where players get to choose what LI they want to romance—these options lead to specific LI endings. Game designers and writers Josiah Lebowitz and Chris Klug also recommend that "if you can think of two or more very interesting ways for the story to end or you want to challenge players," designing a couple of endings can encourage players to strategize getting the better outcome and experiment with different choices, skills, relationships, etc., to try and get it.[19]

In a moment, I'll discuss endings that are specific to NPCs or love interests (LIs). Endings often wrap up a subplot or character arc; therefore, they should have a resolution or feel as if that part of the story has truly come to an end. So, if the MC has won the heart of an LI, the ending should clearly depict them in a relationship. (Or, if the LI is a character who has been unlucky in love, hurt before, or hard to get, it should be obvious that the LI is open to being in a relationship.) This doesn't mean that there can't be *bad* endings! The player may end up on a villain's or antagonist's route, or makes choices that lead to the accumulation of one or more negative consequences. The key is that the ending is *satisfying* in that it has a logical conclusion and feels complete. Can the player see how all of the elements in the story, including their choices, led them to that ending? Based on their character's circumstances at the end of the game, they may or may not be happy with where the MC ends up, but they should be able to understand how they got there and how the story resolved.

Players may have spent hours engaging with the story—they should experience an end to at least one of its conflicts, including when that conflict = the pursuit of an LI.

Endings should be distinct from one another. If you've ever played a game where the endings have a line or two of dialogue changed between them, you'll probably agree that those didn't feel like separate endings.[20] Now, if you spend an extra 20+ hours replaying the game to get a different ending, you may have been extremely disappointed, and your opinion may have even soured on the game. It's totally okay to think like a player when you're designing or writing. How would you, as a player, respond to the endings you're envisioning? Does the player-character or MC's fate feel distinct in each ending? Do the fates of other characters'?

Another way you can think about endings is that they're mini stories at the end of a much larger story. A common complaint about endings is that they can feel uneven. Some endings are shorter, which can make them feel like an afterthought. If every ending is its own developed scenario, it can feel more balanced. Giving each ending the same number of emotional beats is a way to even them out.

The Walking Dead: Season Two centers around an intense, climactic scene between Kenny and Jane and three choices the player can make as Clementine to resolve the adults' violent fight. The endings, each a complete story, then branch as the game's denouement.

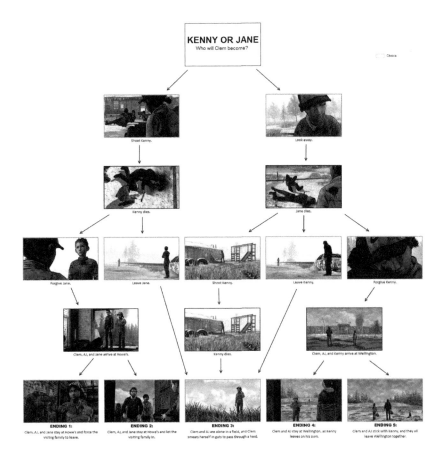

CAPTION: RaiderGuy, "Here's a flowchart I made of all the possible endings," Reddit, last accessed April 25, 2022, https://www.reddit.com/r/TheWalkingDeadGame/comments/2erqla/s2e5_spoilers_heres_a_flowchart_i_made_of_all_the/.

The player must decide whether to shoot Kenny (and kill him) to keep him from killing Jane or let him kill Jane. Once the fight is over, the player can stay with Kenny or Jane or choose for Clementine to take newborn AJ with her and leave the surviving adult behind. If Clementine stays with Kenny or Jane, there are two branching scenarios off of these endings. Each of the two scenarios features their own conflicts and resolutions to end the game. Whether Clementine ends up alone with AJ, stays with Jane, or stays with Kenny, these are very different mini stories but they're balanced because they all have plots, dramatic tension, and emotional beats.

"True"/"Good" and "Bad" Endings

A common convention in choice-based games is to label endings "true" or "good" and "bad." The game's developer considers the true ending to be the canon ending. Noncanonical endings are labeled something like "Ending 1 of 5," or another naming system that signals to the player that they're not canon. Bad and good endings correlate to ethical/moral choices and behaviors, or "bad" is another way to label a noncanonical ending, while "good" is canon. Depending on your story, you might not want to use this practice. If the endings are not tied to a morality system,[21] then calling them "bad" places a judgment on them that players might disagree with. Players may prefer noncanonical endings. An ending is more than just how the story wraps up in a final scenario. It's the culmination of the player's interactions in the world you've created, all the choices they made and the emotional ups and downs those choices elicited in them, and their emotional involvement with the story and characters. Labeling those playthroughs "noncanonical" invalidates them and makes everything the player experienced less meaningful and impactful.

However, labeling endings "true" or "good" and "bad" can be an effective strategy. This should be purposeful with a *reason* for doing so, not just because it's a convention. When players get the good ending, it means they can play again to get the bad ending. (This is similar to numbering endings "1 of 5," "2 of 5," etc., because it tells the player there are five endings in total, and they can try to get any they missed.) Calling an ending "true" signals to the player that they have finally gotten the ending that ties all arcs together if they don't get it on their first playthrough, and if it's an ending that ties all subplots and arcs together, players usually *can't* get it during their first playthrough. Important plot points and character development can be spread along multiple routes and endings. Part of the gameplay is having to play through the game multiple times to get all or most of the endings and seeing how all mysteries tie together in the overarching plot. Revelations in other playthroughs finally weave together as the full picture is completed.

"True" endings work in stories like *999: Nine Hours, Nine Persons, Nine Doors* because each "non-true" ending is a timeline that reveals more of the story. Writer Kotaro Uchikoshi describes this as the player-character having the same abilities as the player (traversing branches), so they can jump from different timelines and visit the past and future.[22] Along these timelines (branches), the player gets clues and mysteries solved in other plot and character arcs. The true ending is reliant upon knowledge of other endings because it is a culmination of all the other arcs, not simply one of several different endings the player can unlock. In this way, *999*'s branching structure is a foundational part of its narrative design and storytelling. The branching itself is a part of the story. You may also think of clever ways to use the very structure of branching in your story's plot.

Secret Endings

Secret or hidden endings are extremely difficult to get. Usually, a certain combination of choices and variables are involved, and sometimes the player must have already played through the game and gotten certain endings. There are a number of reasons you might include one or more secret endings. They can add humor to more serious games, showing characters in unexpected lights, or serve as alternate endings. They can be a reward for player exploration, like revisiting locations multiple times, exhausting all of the options in the dialogue tree, attempting to discover other secrets in the game, finding all items or lore, etc. There are players who try to 100% games and find *everything*, so secret endings are that very special content only they are privy to.

I mentioned that I designed secret endings for *Siren Song* in "The Visual Novel Audience." And I designed them specifically for those who like to play through a visual novel multiple times. Some of the choices players have to make to get the secret endings are earlier in the game, some come later, and one is a premium choice. Since the VN is a free-to-play game, players have to use diamonds (the in-app currency) to make one of these choices. In selecting all of these choices, players would automatically get locked into the secret ending. My idea was that players would have to do some experimenting to find the secret endings, but once they got one of the endings, they could see how the choices logically led to it.

Hatoful Boyfriend's Hidden Lore

Secret endings can also serve as true endings in that they deliver major revelations. In *Hatoful Boyfriend: A School of Hope and White Wings*, the MC, Hiyoko, is a human teenaged girl living in a world where very few humans exist. Anthropomorphic birds about half the size of humans are now the dominant species, and Hiyoko goes to St. Pigeonation's Institute, a high school with several pigeon boys she can romance. The game is fun and lighthearted, but there are several clues in the environments and story suggesting that this is a distant future where humans were nearly wiped out.

CAPTION: Remnants of human civilization in *Hatoful Boyfriend*. © Mediatonic. Jarenth, "Indie Wonderland: *Hatoful Boyfriend*," *Ninja Blues* (blog), November 10, 2014, http://www.ninja-blues.com/2014/11/10/indie-wonderland-hatoful-boyfriend/2/.

Players must unlock most of the other endings before they can get the secret ending—which reveals the fate of humanity and that this is a postapocalyptic world, and how birds took over. Revelatory lore doesn't have to be saved for secret endings, but unlocking such shocking or surprising information in its own coherent story is, naturally, more gripping and engaging for players than finding or being given bits of that lore and having to piece it together to make sense of it.

LIs' and Other Characters' Endings

Games can end focusing on LIs and other NPCs. Character endings should resolve a conflict between the MC and NPC, or the MC and NPC overcome an external conflict. In dating sims, when the player romances one LI, the game can lock into that specific character's route. The character route now becomes the main branch[23] where their relationship with the MC develops for good or ill, and the player gets that LI's specific ending. If your game has LIs that the player can pursue, each LI needs at least one ending. LIs can also have a good ending (the relationship is in a good place by game's end) or a bad ending (the relationship is strained or doesn't work out by game's end). For endings that aren't based on LIs and romance, players can lock into a character's ending by taking that character's side over other NPCs, being nice to or befriending the character, or having the right variables for that character (a job, completing certain events or quests, skill levels, etc.), among other things.

A character Hiyoko befriends features in a couple of *Hatoful Boyfriend's* non-LI endings. To get Azami's ending, Hiyoko has to accept a job at Torimi Cafe. When Hiyoko is out late one night, she's confronted by punkgeons. Azami, a sparrow who's a fierce fighter, helps Hiyoko fight them off. In an act of gratitude, Hiyoko invites Azami to Torimi, where she has later interactions with Azami and becomes her protégé. The two endings based on this relationship include Hiyoko finding out about Azami's long-lost love and Azami declaring Hiyoko a "true sparrow," and they start a biker gang.[24] Like other types of endings, character-specific ones can also be revelatory with secrets and insights into where characters' relationships stand by the end of the game or how they evolve (positively or negatively) in "ever after" scenarios.

DESIGNING HOW PLAYERS UNLOCK ENDINGS

Here's a partial list to help you design branching that results in multiple endings. There are a number of ways players can unlock endings, whether they are normal or secret:

- Via a specific choice or number of specific choices.
- Via choices selected in a particular sequence.
- By using in-app, premium currency to make choices or unlock content.
- With specific variables, like skill levels, abilities acquired, inventory items, etc.
- With a combination of specific choices and variables.
- By solving specific puzzles.
- Through character relationships (good, bad, or neutral).
- With specific events or quests completed.
- By reaching certain endings to unlock new endings.

OUTLINING THE STORY: SOME TECHNIQUES

Designers can outline using the same techniques that they would for linear stories. However, this can be tricky because if you start with a linear story and try to add branches, some branches may feel unbalanced. This can erroneously signal to players that there is only one "correct path," and those other routes don't have equal weight or the same amount of emotional resonance, Sam Maggs notes.[25] Approaching outlining branching structures from different angles can make tackling them easier.

Start with the Ending(s): What happens in each ending? What happens in the story leading up to this point in order to make each ending a reality? The major plot points and emotional beats influencing endings are potential branches leading to that ending.

Start with Character Fates: These are not necessarily endings. Characters can move in and out of a story for a number of reasons: death, breaking off a friendship or romance, etc. Where do their individual stories end, and what happens to lead to this result?

Determine Where Players Will Learn Key Information: Whether they're putting together a mystery or trying to understand the motivations of an NPC, players will be constantly learning important information. There can be branches where they learn this critical information. If getting a complete picture of the overarching narrative requires more than one playthrough, think about how unlocking each ending will reveal more pieces of the puzzle.

Consider Character-Specific Routes: Once a player locks into a character's route, are other NPCs no longer a part of the story? If they're not, you won't have to design interactions for them. If they are a part of the story, how present are they? What is their relationship with the character whose route the player is on? The character-specific route can branch in a variety of ways based upon that character's relationships with the MC and other NPCs.

Design Character-Specific Routes as Main Branches/Stories: When players are locked into the character-specific route, it is now the main branch of the story. Design it as you would other main branches with a main plot arc, main character arcs for the MC and the character at the heart of the route, and points where branches will diverge and rejoin the main branch.

Think about Actions Players Will Want to Take at Certain Moments: Forecasting how players will want to behave and having "a strong sense of the most common and/or meaningful actions they will want to take is important. If you have a divisive NPC for example, the type who some players will want to hug and others will want to punch, forcing everyone into one reaction or another at a key moment will guarantee that half of your player base will be frustrated."[26]

Feedback will be especially helpful once you have an outline, flowchart, or other way of diagramming the branching structure. You may not see where you haven't given elements of the story equal weight, like branches, character arcs, emotional beats, endings, etc. There can also be continuity errors where branches don't reconnect to the main story or places where you haven't indicated how certain variables lead to conditional routes or branches. If you're working within a writing or narrative design team, and everyone on the team has a hand in designing the branching narrative, it is better to find someone outside of the team who can review the design. Everyone on the team is too close to the work and may not see potential problem areas or be able to give insight into how to strengthen the design.

EXERCISES

1. Design a Simple Branching Structure

   Design a simple branching structure with two branches and one ending.

   Now, add parameters to your structure.

   - How does the player unlock each branch? Is it through choices or other variables? Add the choices or variables to your diagram.

2. Design a Complex Branching Structure

   Design a branching structure with (1) at least two branches, (2) nested branches diverging off of each branch, and (3) at least two endings.

   - Make some of your branches conditional by adding variables. Try to design different types of variables than you did in Exercise 1.

NOTES

1 Paul Nelson, "Designing Branching Narrative," *The Story Element* (blog), February 11, 2015, https://thestoryelement.wordpress.com/2015/02/11/designing-branching-narrative/.

2 Ibid.

3 Ibid.

4 Sam Kabo Ashwell, "Standard Patterns in Choice-Based Games," *These Heterogenous Tasks* (blog), January 26, 2015, https://heterogenoustasks.wordpress.com/2015/01/26/standard-patterns-in-choice-based-games/.

5 Ibid.

6 Ibid.

7 Ibid.

8 You can track variables in story scripting languages and game engines, but you need to document these variables *before* you begin scripting. It's very easy to lose track of them and have broken branches because of it.

9 Graham Reznick, Sam Maggs, Karin Weekes, Sam Barlow, and Christian Divine, "Developing Branching Narratives: LudoNarraCon 2020 Panel," April 25, 2020, YouTube video, 48:05, https://www.youtube.com/watch?v=mgD81pQlu1o.

10 Ibid.

11 Unless you have hours upon hours of time to waste, I highly recommend *not* visiting TV Tropes. It is a timesuck (although a highly entertaining one).

12 "Story Branch Favoritism," TV Tropes, accessed April 24, 2022, https://tvtropes.org/pmwiki/pmwiki.php/Main/StoryBranchFavoritism.

13 Graham Reznick, Sam Maggs, Karin Weekes, Sam Barlow, and Christian Divine, "Developing Branching Narratives: LudoNarraCon 2020 Panel," April 25, 2020, YouTube video, 48:05, https://www.youtube.com/watch?v=mgD81pQlu1o.

14 Cass Phillips, "All Choice No Consequence: Efficiently Branching Narrative," Game Developers Conference 2016, uploaded December 12, 2019, YouTube video, 30:14, https://www.youtube.com/watch?v=TEa9aSDHawA.

15 Ibid.

16 Gates lock certain content from players or keep them from progressing in the game if they don't meet specific requirements.

17 These branches are called "conditional branches" because a condition must be met for the player to unlock their content. That condition is a specific variable.

18 Josiah Lebowitz and Chris Klug, *Interactive Storytelling for Video Games: A Player-Centered Approach for Creating Memorable Characters and Stories* (Burlington, Focal Press, 2011), 151.

19 Ibid.

20 If the game touts itself as having multiple endings, then this would be false advertising. However, games can have one main ending, and variables might determine how scenarios are a little different from each other. For example, the player-character gets away with a crime in the game's one ending. Whether they are plagued with guilt the rest of their life or are guilt free is dictated by variables and can be told in a line or two.

21 A mechanic in which a game judges choices and actions as either good or bad/evil. The game tracks the player's choices and actions and unlocks or gates content, including endings, based on how "good" or "bad" the player-character is.

22 Kotaro Uchikoshi, "Visual Novels: Narrative Design in *Virtue's Last Reward*," Game Developers Conference 2013, uploaded July 1, 2018, YouTube video, 54:12, https://www.youtube.com/watch?v=vrxz3s0L8F8.

23 Michelle Clough, message to author, April 25, 2022.

24 Various contributors, "Azami Koshiba," Hatoful Boyfriend Wiki, accessed April 27, 2022, https://hatoful.fandom.com/wiki/Azami_Koshiba.

25 Graham Reznick, Sam Maggs, Karin Weekes, Sam Barlow, and Christian Divine, "Developing Branching Narratives: LudoNarraCon 2020 Panel," April 25, 2020, YouTube video, 48:05, https://www.youtube.com/watch?v=mgD81pQlu1o.

26 Michelle Clough, message to author, April 25, 2022.

CHAPTER 8

Choice and Consequence Design

Actions and Reactions

O NE OF THE MOST vital characteristics of choice-based games is, in fact, their choices. Choices create the branching. They give players things to say and do when there aren't other mechanics, and they are a fundamental way in which players assert their agency. Both great and bad choices make games memorable, but for very different reasons. Here, we'll look at approaches we can take in designing and writing satisfying choices.

CHOICE DESIGN

One of the biggest criticisms players have with choice-based games is the dissatisfaction with the choices themselves. They often feel writers force them to "like" certain love interests and that they are punished for pursuing others. Another problem is that players are faced with Hobson's choices (non-choices). They also feel their choices have no

DOI: 10.1201/9781003199724-10

effect on the story, as "Choices don't matter" is a common refrain. Here's a quick primer about good choice design, how to add choices in scenes to enhance player agency, and how to seed consequences based on choices throughout the story.

Types of Choices to Avoid or to Use Sparingly

These types of choices aren't necessarily *bad*, but they might frustrate players, if you have too many options like these in your game.

Meaningless Choices: The story world should respond to the player's choice in some way, even if the player chooses what the main character (MC) wears. For example, the player chooses a leather jacket. The MC's character art changes to reflect that they're now wearing a leather jacket. Or, at some point, the story should reference the leather jacket in the text, or at least another character needs to acknowledge the jacket. Players need to experience their choices, or they'll wonder why there's a point to making them.

Uninformed/Confusing Choices: Players have no idea what the options will lead to or what the immediate consequences (positive or negative) will be. Some surprises are good, but the player should be able to forecast to a certain degree what might happen based on what they choose. This is only in relation to the immediate consequence of a choice. Choices can lead to long-term consequences that arise later (or much later) in the story. (More on consequences later in this chapter.)

One-Choice Options: These simply transition the player from one part of the story to the next or a new location. One-choice options tend to be an action or line of dialogue that the MC can do or say without the player making a decision. One-choice options are, effectively, a "Continue" or "Next" button.

    For example,

    Let's go!

Synonymous Choices: It's difficult for the player to see a difference between the given options. It's as if both choices are the same, but the prompts are written a little differently. Additionally, there's little difference between what the MC does or says in each choice's branch, further emphasizing that the choices are basically the same.

For example, the player has these dialogue options:

"I can do this alone."

"I can do this by myself."

Let's say these dialogue choices are intended to show different aspects of the MC's personality and how he feels toward the character he's addressing. The problem is that a player may sense the same attitude from "do this alone" and "do this by myself." The differences in choice prompts can't be too subtle. Players need to understand what they're choosing. The dialogue options are more distinct if they read like this:

"I don't *want* your help."

"I can do this on my own."

Now, it's clear that the first choice is cold toward the character the MC is addressing, and the second is more emotionally neutral. Players can posit that the other character will have a negative reaction to the first choice.

Hobson's Choices: A Hobson's choice is "an apparently free choice when there is no alternative."[1] "Take it, or leave it" and "Do it, or don't" are examples of this because these choices only offer the player one real choice, where the other choice is an illusion. Hobson's choices force players to make the "take it" or "do it" choice. The unviable choice usually, in players' minds, turns out to waste their time because the branching narrative rejoins the main story and forces them to take the actual choice. Hobson's choices can be extremely frustrating for players because they feel tricked into making a choice they didn't want, or they wonder why they had the second option in the first place.

For example, the player has these options:

Take the elevator.

Take the stairs.

Let Miguel decide.

The first choice prompt leads to this scenario:

Take the elevator.

We rushed to the elevator. There was an "Out of Order" sign posted on the doors.

Miguel sighed and rolled his eyes.

"Guess we're taking the stairs," I said.[2]

The second prompt leads to this scenario:

Take the stairs.

The stairs were always cluttered with trash, but it was better than waiting for that ancient elevator.

"After you," I said as I opened the door to the stairwell.

The third prompt leads to this scenario:

Let Miguel decide.

"I don't trust the elevator even works," Miguel said.

"Stairs it is," I said. "I didn't get my steps in today anyway."

The stairs were always cluttered with trash, but it was better than waiting for that ancient elevator.

"After you," I said as I opened the door to the stairwell.

Whether to take the stairs or the elevator or to let Miguel make the choice is a minor decision in this instance, but the only real choice here is to take the stairs. The choices redirect the player back to the stairs. This is annoying to players because they'll probably wonder, "Well, why is this even a choice if I can't go down the elevator?" Illusory choices like these become even *more* annoying when players get excited for a choice option, and then they find out it doesn't lead anywhere.

Strong Choices

These types of choices are stronger in their design because they challenge players, they facilitate player agency in giving players the ability to express how they view the MC's personality, and they influence the story's plot and character arcs immediately and later on.

Difficult Choices: Difficult choices are great! These can present awesome options the player has a hard time choosing, heartbreaking options the player agonizes over (or gets emotionally involved in), and options the players know will bring the MC trouble whatever they decide.

Choices with Long-Term Consequences: Strong choices lead to immediate consequences that players experience right away, but they also have consequences that may affect characters, the world, or the plot in ways players may not foresee later in the story. These long-term consequences make players' choices feel even more meaningful, as the story will continue to respond to their decisions. Knowing their decisions may have long-term consequences, players are more likely to weigh the cost of each option before choosing one.

"Nonjudgmental" Choices: The choices don't present "right" and "wrong" options, nor does the writer seem to inject their own opinion or moral judgment based on what the player chooses. A common issue players raise is the sense that the writer wants them to make certain choices, whether they are plot-based or character-driven. They feel writers judge and punish them if they don't choose the "right" love interest or make the "wrong" decision. A nonjudgmental choice doesn't mean that it won't lead to negative consequences, but any consequence should feel like a natural story progression, not that the player is being penalized.

Choices Revealing Different Facets of the MC's Personality: The options you give can show off different parts of the MC's personality. For example, one dialogue option might be more sarcastic, while the other is a little more forgiving. Letting players determine the MC's personality and characterization facilitates the players' ability to roleplay.

For example,

"You *should* blame yourself!"

"Stop beating yourself up."

Players can see that the character the MC is addressing will have very different responses to these dialogue choices, and the choices will likely alter the characters' relationship to some degree. At the same time, the options show two sides of the same MC. The MC can be both sympathetic and caring ("Stop beating yourself up") and unsympathetic and unforgiving ("You *should* blame yourself!").

Unlockable Choices: These are choices based on variables. The MC must have a particular stat, skill, etc., or they unlock the choice in another way, like helping one non-player character (NPC) over another. These choices are linked directly to players' earlier decisions. In mobile games, these can also be premium choices. They're the "superior" option, where the other choice(s) lead to content that is less exciting.

BRANCHING NARRATIVE AND CONSEQUENCES

We know how important it is to facilitate an experience where players feel like they're driving the story. Player agency is an important part of giving players a sense that they're in control of the narrative. But there's another important part of that equation, and that's how the world reacts and the consequences that result from those reactions. That might sound contradictory. How can the player drive the story if the world reacts to player choices, especially if the world reacts unfavorably or presents challenges to those decisions?

An involving, engaging, worthwhile experience wouldn't seem as real if NPCs didn't have certain thoughts and feelings about the MC's behavior and/or what was going on in their own worlds. Choices players make wouldn't feel as monumental if they had no tangible effects that players could witness and experience.

We need to design consequences into our stories, and those consequences have to be believable.

What Is a Consequence?

We tend to use "consequences" as a negative term: "You're going to have to face the consequences of your actions." The term "consequences" in a design sense, however, is neutral.

"Consequence" is made of the prefix "con," meaning "with" or "together," and "*sequi*," meaning to follow. So, "consequence" literally means "that which follows from or grows out of any act or course."[3]

"That which follows from or grows out of any act or course" is pretty broad. Which means that the consequences we design for player choices can facilitate a range of experiences, too.

Why Consequences Are Important

They Make the Story More Interesting and Involving: If we're exerting our influence over a world, and a game *does* have a world, then we should see what effects our choices are having on that world. If people know we bomb a town, they need to whisper about us with derision as we pass by. Or, if they were enemies of that town, they will speak of us as a hero.

They Make the Game More Challenging: When NPCs don't agree with the player's choices, they can make life difficult for the MC in any number of ways. Resistance makes things more challenging and gives the player a deeper emotional journey.

We don't always know how the world and NPCs will react to choices and what benefits or problems that might bring. Some choices should be predictable. Players should have an idea of what's going to happen as a consequence to some choices.

They Make the World More Alive and Believable: If we're influencing someone's world or life, they're going to have strong feelings about that. Expressing those feelings is only natural.

Consequences and the World

Players need to see the effects of their choices manifest in the world. Those manifestations can happen in a number of ways.

The physical world may be altered, like the player gaining or losing access to an area or location. This could be because the MC has the right relationship with an NPC. The player may choose to *destroy* an area, meaning the MC is literally responsible for losing access to part of the world.

NPCs might become hostile or helpful toward a player. *Until Dawn* has multiple player-characters. In Chapter 6, the antagonist forces the player-as-Chris to choose whether to shoot Ashley (someone he's attracted to, and the feeling is mutual), shoot himself, or choose not to shoot at all. No matter what Chris chooses, he and Ashley survive. However, if Chris tries to shoot Ashley, she will harbor a deep resentment toward him from that moment on, and their relationship stat drops to zero. The long-term consequence of the player-as-Chris choosing Ashley to die manifests in Chapter 8.[4] A wendigo chases the player-as-Chris through the woods. As he approaches the safety of the lodge, Ashley will shut the door on him, leaving the wendigo to tear Chris to pieces outside. This is a major consequence (losing a player-character for the rest of the game), but minor consequences are effective storytelling tools, too.

Major vs. Minor Consequences

When thinking about designing consequences, you can go big, or you can go small. But consequences still make an impact because they reflect the player's choices.

Major consequences, to name a few, are removing or adding characters, removing or adding levels/locations, removing or adding events/quests/missions, improving or hurting relationships that influence the overall story.

Minor consequences are removing or adding dialogue options, making references based on player-character attributes, making references to or NPCs stating directly their perspectives on MCs and their choices, and improving or hurting relationships that don't influence the overall story. In the first *Life Is Strange*, the rewind mechanic allows MC Max to open up new dialogue options. When she learns something from an NPC, she can rewind time and bring it up as if she knew about it all along. This information doesn't change the story on a fundamental level, but it often increases her relationships with characters or gives her (and the player by extension) a better understanding of or appreciation for the NPC she's talking to.

NPC Reactions to Consequences

We've covered NPC reactions a little bit already (notably Ashley saving Chris or letting him die). It wouldn't be believable if NPCs didn't have reactions to player choices, especially when they care about what the player is doing, or the player affects them directly.

It makes sense that, when they're displeased, NPCs would provide some pushback from those that inhabit the world or provide aid when they approve of the player's actions. However NPCs respond, it should be believable for their characters' makeup. In Ashley's case, she does care about Chris. If she chooses to leave him to die, she's disturbed by her own decision, even as she treats him with cruelty. NPCs can act out of character just as easily as an MC can, so their reactions have to be believable to players.

PLOTTING CONSEQUENCES

Where, exactly, should the consequence (or consequences) of a player's choice pop up? Does the consequence lead to new choices that lead to even more consequences?

You've got lots of flexibility here, but the player's confrontation with the consequence should feel natural. And even if the player is surprised by the consequence, if they think about it, they should be able to say, "Yeah, it makes sense that it went down this way."

Add Consequences Immediately after the Choice: There's a cause, and there's an immediate effect. Whether or not there's a later consequence, players need immediate feedback on their decisions. Players can usually figure out what an immediate consequence will be. Think of those situations where we have good relationships with two NPCs, and a choice we have to make is going to piss off one of them, and we really, really, *really* don't want to hurt either of them. That's a predictable consequence, but it's still effective.

When Players Don't Experience an Immediate Consequence after a Choice … : A warning if you plot out consequences to not be an immediate effect of a choice: Players may feel like their choice was meaningless because they did not experience an immediate response.

Seeding Consequences

We can seed a consequence or multiple consequences to a choice throughout the story.

For example, whether or not Chris lives or dies in Chapter 8 of *Until Dawn* has a profound effect on the rest of the game. If Chris is alive, he appears in more scenes and has interactions with other characters, and his relationship stats with these characters change. If Ashley is alive in her ending, what she says about Chris changes based on whether he died due to the player's inability to get him to the lodge safely (the player decides to not shoot Ashley) or she's the reason he dies. There are a number of ways the story can branch based on whether Chris is alive or dead.

Seeding Builds Tension/Conflict: I wrote a text-based story where a choice the player makes early creates a consequence that leads to a later consequence at the end of the story. The story is told in chapters. In Chapter 2, the MC can delete some communications or not. In the very last chapter, the MC can decide to use those communications as proof against her antagonist. At this point in the story, the MC is under a lot of pressure, and those communications can help her get out of a bad situation.

I designed these choices and consequences thinking that, in a very emotional moment, the player may have forgotten that they deleted the communications all those chapters ago. (Or they may remember that they *didn't* delete them, and they have a way out of that bad situation.)

Add Consequences When It's Natural for the NPC's Character Arc: NPCs are on their own journeys, and they have their own story arcs. When are they motivated to act? When are they motivated by the player's choice? Think about how someone in your life has responded to something you've done, whether they were happy or angry about it. They may have held a grudge for a long time and suddenly seemed to explode out of nowhere, like Ashley's cruelty toward Chris. Or maybe you did something kind for someone, and years later, after you forgot about it, they showed their appreciation.

Think about NPCs who are affected by the player's choices, what their responses would be, and *when* their responses would be.

CONSEQUENCES AND SCOPE

Whatever consequences you design, they must remain within your game's scope. They have to be within budget and the game's technological constraints. The more choices and consequences you design and write, the more scenes you'll need for them. Are you adding locations to the world through these choices and consequences? Are you adding more characters, or even more character art and/or animations for existing characters? Do you need to hire more writers and/or artists to implement your plans? If you do need more assets, do you have the budget for them?

Along with budget constraints, a very real issue is schedule. If you have an inflexible schedule for your game's development, you may not have time to include complicated branching based on consequences. (And you could run out of money before all of your plans make it into the game.) Consider what you do and don't have time for.

Find out from your team if your ideas are going to be feasible.

DETERMINING AN NPC'S RESPONSE-AS-CONSEQUENCE

To recap …

These questions can help you think about how an NPC might feel about a player's choice and whether that might lead to a consequence:

- How does the player's choice impact the NPC's life?
- Does the choice change the NPC's perception of the MC, for good or ill?
- What's important to the NPC?
- How does the player's choice impact the lives of those the NPC cares about?
- Are the NPC and MC allies or at odds?
- Does the NPC see the player's choice as intentionally or unintentionally harming them? (What is the level of offense?)
- Does the NPC see the player's choice as intentionally or unintentionally helping them? (What is the level of gratitude?)

HOW WILL THE PLAYER EXPERIENCE CONSEQUENCES?

When you're designing consequences, think about how the player will experience them. Every choice will manifest in the world for good or ill, even if it's a small thing that influences just the MC and/or one other character and no one else. The bigger the consequence attached to the choice, the bigger the reaction(s) should be.

What Reactions Can Be:

A Physical Sign of the Player's Choice: The player chooses what the MC wears, and the MC's character art changes to reflect the choice. Or perhaps the player engages in a criminal act. They must avoid the scene of the crime. That location now has crime tape up, and the MC can't physically go there.

NPCs Speak Directly to the MC about the Choice: This can be an immediate reaction, or they can bring it up later (or much later) in conversation or other means of communication.

The Player Hears NPCs Talking about It: If your game has ambient dialogue through sound assets or pop-up text boxes,[5] players can see or read how the inhabitants are responding to a choice. This can also be done through a narrator, where scene building or summarizing describes what people are saying.

The Player Sees Evidence of the Choice in Other Places: The player can read about choices they've made in lore, on menu screens, or in logs/journals chronicling the story.

Remember that one choice can have more than one consequence, and you can seed these consequences throughout the main story, the plot arc of a particular branch, or a character route. When there is an NPC reaction to these consequences, keep their responses consistent with their personalities, desires, and motives.

If you have a team, involve them in the design of the game's choices and consequences. This will help you stay within scope and budget, and you won't waste your energy planning something that's not feasible.

EXERCISE

Designing and Adding Consequences

Use the second exercise from "Designing Branching Narratives." This is a branching structure with (1) at least two branches, (2) nested branches diverging off of each branch, and (3) at least two endings.

1. Add immediate consequences to every choice, if you don't already have choices.

   - How does each choice lead to the specific consequence?

   - Has the player altered the world in some way or changed some aspect of the MC?

   - Are these consequences NPC reactions?

2. Add one or more consequences that result much later from the initial choices you have designed in Part 1.

   - How does each new consequence naturally arise from the initial choice and consequence?

   - Do these consequences benefit the player or introduce a challenge? How?

NOTES

1 "Hobson's choice," Merriam-Webster, accessed May 5, 2022, https://www.merriam-webster.com/dictionary/Hobson'schoice.

2 Sometimes, when a game adds insult to injury, there's editorializing that the player should have taken the other option: "I *told* you we should have taken the stairs," Miguel said under his breath.

3 "Consequence," Online Etymology Dictionary, accessed May 5, 2022, https://www.etymonline.com/word/consequence.

4 Various Contributors, "Ashley and Chris," *Until Dawn* Wiki, accessed May 5, 2022, https://until-dawn.fandom.com/wiki/Ashley_and_Chris.

5 Dialogue spoken by NPCs who are usually not important to the story (i.e., they're not main, secondary, or even tertiary characters) and triggered as the player explores the world. The player does not have to interact with NPCs to hear or read ambient dialogue.

CHAPTER 9

Character Development and Routes

Writing MCs and NPCs

I DISCUSS THE ART OF character design in "Developing Your Own Visual Novels and Interactive Fiction: A Quick Guide." Here, I want to cover the design of a character in relationship to its involvement in the story. This includes the benefits of using archetypes to establish roles, personality makeups, and interactions with other characters; choosing the right point of view for the main character, character arcs for both the main story and character-specific routes; and writing LIs.

USING ARCHETYPES

Using straight **archetypes**[1] can make characters stereotypical or caricatured, even if you're writing a parody or satire. Another major flaw of archetypes is that they can make stories predictable. Players become well versed in these archetypes the more they play visual novels. Story genres, like fantasy, noir, high school romance, etc., also have their own character

DOI: 10.1201/9781003199724-11

archetypes. Players can identify an archetype in a character, based upon the game being a VN and its setting within a certain story genre, and that archetype signifies that the character will have a specific role in the story. Players know how parts of the story are going to unfold as soon as they're introduced to that archetypal character.

However, there are benefits to using archetypes. Players have genre expectations. When they play certain types of games, they're going to expect to see thematic elements and characters common to those genres, which players enjoy. At the same time, they want to see something new. If you tweak or subvert archetypes, it will give characters depth, make them more interesting, and make their motives and behaviors more unpredictable and unexpected. If the childhood best friend who's always supported the main character (MC) through trials and tribulations turns out to be assisting the villain, this backstabbing behavior can be an emotionally engaging, rewarding twist.

MC Archetypes

These are some common MC archetypes. It's important to note that a character can be made up of more than one:

- **Everyday Joe or Jane:** A type of "everyperson" whom anyone can relate to. Whether they're in a slice-of-life story or a space opera, they're not remarkable, but the circumstances they find themselves in are. They're also likely to be ciphers (see "The Main Character and Types of MCs" below).

- **Overachiever:** Someone smart and gifted who's gone through life with few challenges, whether they're a high school student or a billionaire looking for love. They can be a bit of a jerk because they believe they're the smartest person in the room. Conflicts in the story will challenge them in ways that make them deeply uncomfortable.

- **Underachiever:** The opposite of the overachiever, they don't apply themselves (but this doesn't mean they aren't smart). They may also be klutzy or bumbling. Conflict pulls out of them skills and the fortitude to be a hero.

- **Investigator/Detective:** The character's responsibility is to literally piece together clues and solve mysteries. **N.B.** The character doesn't have to be an actual detective or investigator by profession. In the *Danganronpa* franchise, for instance, high school students investigate the murders of their peers.

- **Villain-as-Protagonist:** The protagonist turns out to be the villain behind all of the story's events. This should not be obvious, but the player should have the right clues illuminating the protagonist's true nature.

NPC Archetypes

Non-player characters (NPCs) play roles like side character, antagonist, and deuteragonist,[2] but visual novel NPCs can also fall into some classic tropes and archetypes of their own:

- **Childhood Friend:** The person who has been the MC's best friend their entire lives. Depending on their ages, they go to school together or maybe work together. They may also be the secret villain. If the VN is a romance, the childhood friend is 99.9% likely to be an LI.

- **Tsundere:** Based on a trope from Japanese anime, manga, and VNs, tsundere, usually female, vacillate between being mean to and shy/flustered around the MC.

- **Yandere:** Another trope coming from Japanese storytelling. Yandere, usually female, are obsessed with the main character, to the point of being psychotic. They seem sweet and innocent before their obsession grows.

- **Rival:** A character who has a real or imagined rivalry with the MC. That rivalry can relate to work, academics, sports, etc. In romances, they are a rival for the MC's potential LI(s), or they become an LI.

- **Detached/Disinterested:** A character who appears emotionally unattached and unbothered by the MC's or their own troubling circumstances. However, they tend to care deeply for the MC, whether platonically or romantically. This is also another LI archetype.

- **Absolute Jerk:** Not a villain, this character can be verbally abusive or an outright bully to the MC and other characters. They need believable motivations to not be outright caricatures that players want to avoid whenever they're onscreen.

Remember that character archetypes are a good *starting point*. They'll give you foundational knowledge about the types of characters found in VNs and how these types tend to interact with each other. But characters that are archetypes written without nuance will be predictable clichés. Tweaking or subverting archetypes will make for more well-rounded and interesting characters. *Monster Prom's* Liam, for example, is a hipster archetype who rolls his eyes at anything mainstream. He was, however, a member of a K-pop band.

THE MAIN CHARACTER AND TYPES OF MCs

The player will experience the story through one or more main character points of view (POVs). Visual novels offer different kinds of MCs or player-characters. They may be fixed, customizable, a combination of fixed and customizable, or a cipher. Fixed MCs have an identity that cannot be changed. They are written with a definite history, personality, and name. A player can change any number of characteristics of a customizable MC: name, gender identity and pronouns, appearance (clothes, skin tone, height, weight, hairstyle, hair color), and background. As "a combination of fixed and customizable" suggests, this is an MC who has some characteristics that are fixed, and others that are customizable. A cipher is an MC that can be customizable but, most importantly, they don't have a discernible personality or identity. They are truly a stand-in for the player. In a moment, I'll discuss how the MC type and the narrative point of view affect the relationship that the player has with the MC.

Choosing the MC's POV

It might seem like a simple thing, but picking the correct point of view in which to write the MC's inner monologue and observations is a big deal. Whether the MC's narrative voice is first person, second person, or third-person limited, it will have to carry the player through the entire game. The right POV will draw players in. The wrong one will make the MC feel distant and less emotionally interesting. There's no formula for picking the correct POV, but there are factors that enter into a writer's decision-making.

A Quick Rundown of Points of View:

- **First Person ("I"):** In the POV character's head, the reader/player is exposed to how the character observes the world, events, other characters, and themselves: "I took a few steps down the corridor when

I heard a faint scratching. That was enough for me, and I booked it out of that old, abandoned mall, running as fast as my shaking legs could carry me."

- **Second Person ("You"):** The narration follows the actions, thoughts, and emotions of "you" and treats the reader/player as the protagonist: "You took a few steps down the corridor when you heard a faint scratching. That was enough for you, and you booked it out of that old, abandoned mall, running as fast as your shaking legs could carry you."

- **Third-Person Limited ("He"/"She"/"They"/"It"):** The narration follows a single character. Unlike first-person point of view, third limited is "close" to the character, not in their heads: "She took a few steps down the corridor when she heard a faint scratching. That was enough for her, and she booked it out of that old, abandoned mall, running as fast as her shaking legs could carry her."

- **Third-Person Omniscient ("He"/"She"/"They"/"It"):** The narration is god-like and all knowing, and is not hindered by time and space. It can be anywhere and everywhere and is aware of every character's thoughts, actions, and motivations: "She took a few steps down the corridor when she heard a faint scratching. That was enough for her, and she booked it out of that old, abandoned mall, running as fast as her shaking legs could carry her. Her brother texted her again and again, waiting with the car running in the empty parking lot."

Some POVs are more natural for an MC. For a cipher character, second person makes sense because the cipher is a stand-in for the player. Therefore, the narration refers to "you," the individual playing the game and making all of the choices. The cipher is not an established identity in the story's world, so it may not speak with the more confident "I" voice. "You" are narrated your actions as you perform them. Many romance VNs on mobile are written in second person because they give players opportunities to engage with the LIs of their choice. Fixed characters have well-defined identities. Any POV works for them. It depends on how "close" you want the player to feel to them, and there is any number of reasons why you would or would not want them to. For *Siren Song*, I chose first person because the MC is going through a tumultuous rite of passage with her friends, and I want players to see everything through her eyes and feel what she is feeling.

However, third limited might make sense in a game where part of its design is for the player to be more of an observer of the MC's actions. Sections of *999*'s narrative are in third limited for this reason. By its very nature, this is a POV that is supposed to put some distance between the character and the player or reader. It's the equivalent of looking over the player-character's shoulder or having the player-character's back to the player in third-person games. It's a less intimate voice because you're not in the character's head, unlike in first person, and the story is not speaking directly to you, like in second person.

Third omniscient is an unusual choice for an MC's POV because the omniscient narrator sees and knows all as an observer of the world. It narrates what's happening in places where the MC is not, and it can know the thoughts and feelings of other characters. Third omniscient is better suited for moments where you want to pull away from the MC's perspective and give the player a more general sense of what's going on in the story at large.

While there are logical reasons to choose one POV over another, they may not work for the story. I originally wrote *Incarnō: Everything Is Written* in third-person limited, but it just didn't feel right, so I switched it to first person. Sometimes, you just have to go with what works on a gut level. Try out of a couple of POVs to see which reads and feels best.

Multiple MCs?

Choice-based games don't often have multiple MCs or player-characters, but it is a little more common and less innovative than it used to be, *Professor Layton vs. Phoenix Wright: Ace Attorney* (Level-5/Capcom, 2012) and *Game of Thrones: A Telltale Game Series* (2014) being a couple of examples. If your decision to have multiple MCs begins with "That would be cool" or "It's unusual" or "Players don't usually get to play as more than one MC," those MCs still need a *purpose* and *function* within the overall gameplay and story. In *Professor Layton vs. Phoenix Wright*, Layton and Wright's responsibilities are clearly differentiated. Layton investigates and looks for clues, and Wright defends individuals put on trial. *Game of Thrones*'s gameplay mirrors the TV series. The story follows several MCs from one house and how each attempts to navigate political land mines, as the show follows multiple point-of-view characters that start, try to avoid, or alleviate political peril.

But these are two established franchises. How would several MCs benefit your intellectual property (IP) if you included them? Multiple MCs give players access to parts of the story that only one cannot. Spatially, they can be in more than one place. They can explore the same location or space and leave the player with different insights based upon their worldviews, job experiences, personal philosophies, and motivations. MCs with wildly different life experiences will influence how the player sees the world of the game when the player steps into their shoes. They can be incredibly different experiences within the same scene.

They also have different relationships with NPCs. NPCs will interact with each MC differently, giving players better understandings of whom each NPC is, and they may share different bits of key information with each MC. Multiple MCs assist in revealing the overarching narrative in ways one MC cannot. Does this mean that multiple MCs are best suited for mysteries or games involving stories where players must figure out what's going on? No. It's possible for a slice-of-life game to have more than one MC, where the player explores the complexities of their relationships with each other and NPCs from multiple perspectives.

What Is Each MC's Relationship to the Player?

When a choice-based game has one MC, it's easy to define that MC's relationship to the player. They're the one character who serves as the player's eyes and ears. If there is more than one character now serving as the player's eyes and ears, their roles must be clearly defined. Visual novel *The Letter* (2017) is set in the United Kingdom and takes atmospheric Japanese horror films as its inspiration. At the heart of the story is a posh, haunted mansion for sale. The VN has an ambitious seven MCs, each from different walks of life and with different roles in the story. There are seven chapters, one for each main character POV, and players can experience the same events from these different perspectives. Four of the seven MCs are a tight-knit group of friends: Becca, a school teacher from the United Kingdom; Isabella, a realtor from the Philippines, Ash, a detective inspector from the United States; and Zach, an aspiring film director from the United States.[3] Three of these characters are immigrants, which means the player gets a window into their immigrant perspectives as they navigate the world of aristocrats and their history.

Each of the four has different roles within the unfolding horror mystery and in their relationships with each other. As a detective, Ash helps the player put clues about the haunted mansion together. Isabella gives the player the ability to explore the mansion. Zach communicates with the ghost and provides the player insights into why she's haunting the mansion. Becca's interactions in the mansion give the player lore about its sordid and violent history.

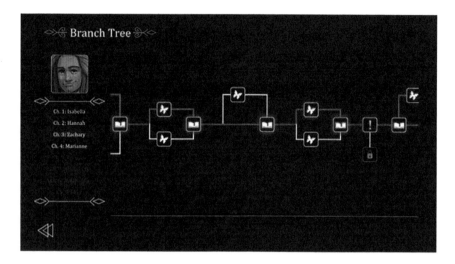

CAPTION: Zach's in-game flowcharts. Developed by Yangyang Mobile and protected by United States and international copyright law. © Yangyang Mobile.

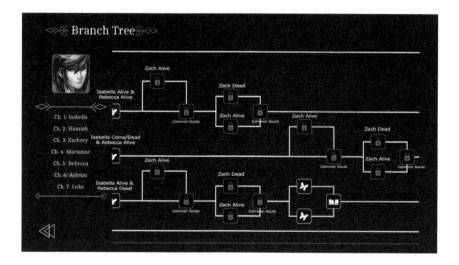

CAPTION: Ash's in-game flowcharts. Developed by Yangyang Mobile and protected by United States and international copyright law. © Yangyang Mobile.

All of these four perspectives are vital to understanding the full history of the mansion and the ghost trapped there. In designing the story's overarching plot, you can decide how each MC fits within the story and then give them a role that reflects their involvement. For example, Ash's is the sixth of seven total chapters. By the time players reach his chapter, they've already received plenty of clues and hints about the history of the mansion and the ghost's haunting. Ash's chapter puts all the clues together, which is befitting of a detective.

Switching MCs and Changing Perspectives

The order of the MCs' perspectives will have a profound influence on how players understand the overall story. The change in perspectives might be linear. The story moves from one MC to the next and does not return to a past MC's perspective (*The Letter*, where each protagonist has one POV chapter), or the story can move back and forth between MCs (*Game of Thrones* and *Until Dawn*). Carefully consider when and why the perspective changes. Does a new MC perspective give added insight? Does the game jump from perspective to perspective to show what's happening to the MCs around the same time? Or does the new perspective conflict with a former one? If the player, in effect, has to choose a side or who's right or wrong, the linear approach may not be the best, as the last POV will be freshest in the player's mind. Switching back and forth between conflicting perspectives challenges players to assess and reassess and analyze carefully what they're learning from each MC.

How Do the MCs' Stories Come Together?

Usually, multiple MCs' stories merge toward the end of or late in the game. If the perspectives move linearly from one to the next, then all of the MCs will probably be present in the climactic scenes, unless there is an MC death. So, consider what scenario brings all of the characters into each others' orbits. Where is the natural point in the overarching plot where all of these stories merge?

PLOTTING WHEN TO SWITCH MC PERSPECTIVES

- Does the game benefit from having more than one MC?
- What is each MC's relationship to the player?
- What is each MC's function within the story?
- How are MCs' relationships with the main NPCs different, and what does the player learn because of these differences?
- Who is the first POV character? The first perspective players have greatly influences how they see the game's world and other characters.
- Who gets the final playable point of view?
- What will be the order of these playable perspectives? How does that order shape and reshape players' perspectives of other characters and their understanding of the overarching plot?
- When in the story does the player jump from one MC to the next? Do they get to choose?

CHARACTER INTERACTIONS

Mileage may vary on how well games illustrate relationships. I think other media have an advantage over games when it comes to displaying and developing relationships. That's because of the way those stories are structured. They tend to have more time to show different facets of several characters' relationships over weeks and months (or hours in the case of films), and that part of the storytelling isn't interrupted by gameplay. VNs have an advantage over other games *because* they're part novel. While a visual novel may not be viewable or playable over months like a TV show, we can get into the heads of characters to see how they're feeling about others. We're able to see the positive and negative parts of relationships with each character, and those relationships define each character as a more complete person. We have descriptions of their emotions, their judgments, and their attractions (romantic and platonic). Because we're in characters' heads, their interactions will seem more intense, funny, or warm in some scenes.

The MC's Relationships with NPCs

We reviewed character archetypes earlier in the chapter. There are certain tropes that grow out of those archetypes, and they serve as a foundation for main characters' relationships with NPCs and NPCs' relationships with each other. These archetypal relationships provide players with a basic understanding of how characters feel about each other and their involvement in each others' lives. Cecilia's friends in *Siren Song* have distinct roles in their relationships with her:

- **Pete**: the older-brother type who gives good advice and keeps everyone grounded;
- **Basyl**: the best friend who cares about the MC despite her flaws and choices, and serves as a potential love interest;
- **Lyle**: the kind-hearted and a-bit-dumb friend who helps the MC keep an optimistic outlook, no matter the odds; and
- **Brandon**: "down to earth" nice guy and potential LI and enemy.

"Potential" is a key word in the list because the player's choices via Cecilia will shape these relationships as the story progresses.

Other relationship archetypes with MCs include (this is certainly not an exhaustive list):

- sworn rivals/enemies (these rivals may or may not have the potential to become LIs, depending on the story and VN subgenre);
- older and younger siblings, where the MC and another character are actual blood relatives or have a sibling-like relationship;
- parent and child (actual blood relatives or like family);
- mentor and mentee (or student and teacher); and
- boss and employee (with the MC usually being the employee).

Like any archetypes, archetypal relationships need to change and grow. This is not only because you want to avoid predictability, but it is also because as characters change and grow, their relationships cannot remain the same.

NPC Relationships with Each Other

NPCs can also have complicated relationships with each other. They can be rivals and outright enemies, especially if they're in competition for the MC's heart. These rivalries can make choices difficult (a *good* thing) because players are forced to take sides or make agonizing decisions one of them won't like, and they know it will result in one of those characters being upset with them.

Other relationship archetypes between NPCs:

- platonic close friends,

- romantic partners,

- siblings,

- parent and child,

- business partners,

- mentor and mentee (or student and teacher), and

- boss and employee.

Monster Prom's dateable[4] characters are all friends, and they're super popular, which means they look down on those who are not. Each character is a type of monster and represents a particular archetype found in society and high school cultures, like a party-girl ghost (Polly) or a dumb-jock werewolf (Scott).

They're monsters, so they engage in activities like extortion, arson, vandalism, and genocide. They do bad things is what I'm saying. But they do have endearing qualities. For example, Liam's belonging to a K-pop band. *Monster Prom* makes it a point to highlight all of the relationships between the dateable monsters, and it's a big part of the game's depth in storytelling.

Julian Quijano, the creative director and a writer for *Monster Prom*, points to the importance of the characters being well rounded, and an essential aspect of that is that they have well-defined relationships with other characters. Below is a slide image from one of Quijano's talks. It illustrates Polly's relationships with the other love interests by focusing on the defining characteristic of each relationship. As Quijano says on the slide: "We're not the same with everyone … Make them real; make them unique; make them spherical."

CAPTION: "Building Chemistry" and "Final Thoughts on *Monster Prom's* Characters."
Beautiful Glitch, "AUGUST UPDATE: so far from home . . . (also, lots of stuff)," Kickstarter, September 12, 2018, https://www.kickstarter.com/projects/corintio/monster-prom/posts/2287300.

So, whenever Polly appears in events with these characters, you can see how her relationships are different with each. With Scott Howl, Polly exhibits her prankster side. Polly and Scott call themselves the "Prank Masterz."

There's even a secret ending and computer graphic (CG) highlighting this relationship.

CAPTION: The "Prank Masterz" CG. Developed by Beautiful Glitch and protected by United States and international copyright law. © Beautiful Glitch.
"PRANK MASTERZ," *Monster Prom* Wiki, last accessed May 2, 2022, https://monster-prom.fandom.com/wiki/PRANK_MASTERZ.

CHARACTER DEVELOPMENT AND CHARACTER ROUTES

Story is a big selling point for visual novels. The characters and how they change as the story progresses is something that endears players to the genre. Characterization and traits may shift, and the player may have a direct hand in this. In writing characters for VNs, we must decide what characters will and won't change, when those changes happen, and how players will experience those changes. Another consideration is which characters will have their own routes, and that will affect the plotting of those character arcs and the overall story.

MC Development

As is the case with other types of games, whether or not the MC will have any character development is an important question. This depends on several factors: the story, the type of MC, the type of VN genre, and its player expectations. So, changes may be large or small: "Sometimes, these changes may be large-scale personality shifts—learning the meaning of heroism/self-sacrifice/self-care/love/etc., and evolving as a character—while some might be micro changes, like falling in love with a specific person or discovering a new hobby."[5]

Ciphers usually don't have character development, since they're avatars for the player. The player projects onto the MC any development they believe the character to be experiencing. Shorter games may not have time for a lot of character development, especially in a short dating sim on mobile, because the point is for the MC to snag the person they're attracted to. Choices show off different parts of the MC's personality, but they're pretty much the same person in the end as when the story began.

Longer, intricately plotted VNs are more likely to have well-rounded protagonists and MC character development, as the protagonist is faced with challenges and conflicts that force them to reevaluate what they believe about the world and themselves, their relationships, and their behavior. Do they find themselves in circumstances where they do things they never would have considered before? With MCs who basically see themselves as "good" people, what darker parts of their personality get pushed into the light by conflicts and opportunities? The same can be asked of MCs who enjoy doing bad things, know they do bad things, and are confronted with being charitable or sacrificial for the benefit of someone else. "Choices," then, "should be key plot beats" where players are "defining the character or [players] are expressing [their] take on the character,"[6] Sam Barlow, the writer and designer of *Her Story* and *Silent Hill* titles, notes.

Choices in these instances give players the opportunity to roleplay and decide whether they favor the more altruistic or selfish aspects of the protagonist, and these decisions can lead to consequential changes in relationships or specific endings. The key is that MCs need to be designed with personalities and motivations that make sense for their actions and any choices the player may make on their behalf. A person who believes stealing is wrong can be enticed to steal when the correct circumstance presents itself.

Tie these personality- and motivation-revealing choices to branching routes that further develop the MC's character. Let's go back to a very short branching narrative from "Designing Branching Narratives": the treasure-hunting MC who decides to steal from their best friend or work with that best friend to find treasure. The "I would never steal from anyone" individual may have the added moral belief that they would certainly not hurt someone they care about like their best friend. But what if they're hundreds of thousands of dollars in debt? Or what if they feel trapped in their job, and they hate the life they're currently living? Sure, they could share with their best friend and pay off some of that debt, or maybe they would have a financial cushion for a year or two while they looked for a new job. *Or* they could take the whole treasure for themselves and pay off all of their debt (with a good chunk left over), or not have to work for years and years. Stealing might be selfish and a betrayal of someone the MC cares about, but the player can understand why the MC might stab their best friend in the back.

For *Siren Song*, I wanted Cecilia to have an internal confrontation about how far she would go to protect herself and her friends or whether she would remain more passive to successfully complete her rite of passage. At a certain age, monsters cross through a veil to the human world to better understand humanity, by disguising themselves as humans and living among them. They are not to use their powers or reveal their true identities. Since they've been monsters their whole lives, it's sometimes difficult to suppress their instincts and true nature. A group of monster hunters lives in the small town where Cecilia and her monster friends are going to high school, and those hunters become aware of the monsters' existence.

The player, through Cecilia, is confronted with killing one of these hunters late in the story, someone whom she befriended. The added pressure is that if she *doesn't* keep the existence of monsters becoming known, the monster world can be jeopardized if humanity discovers it. In this "kill or let live" choice, players have to weigh the emotional connection between Cecilia and the NPC, her desire to keep her monster friends alive, and her fear of surviving or not. This decision leads to several endings— whether or not humanity finds out about monsters, whether or not she spends the rest of her life free or in captivity, or whether Cecilia spends the rest of her life running from a former friend who vows to avenge the monster hunter's death. This choice is possible because Cecilia has a nature to kill, she's proud of the world of monsters from which she comes, she loves her friends, and she's come to care for humans who might wish to kill her if they knew who she really was. At this point, the player decides what's ultimately most important to Cecilia.

Before giving players choices that will reveal aspects of the MC's personality and send them along a route that will develop their character in a particular direction, illustrate and foreshadow aspects of the MC's makeup that will allow them to make certain choices. Choices, just like dialogue and things characters do, should never feel out of character. If they're out of character, they will take players out of the moment and may frustrate them because the choices are unbelievable.

NPCs and Character Development

Just as players can experience MCs changing for better or worse, they can also see NPCs develop—and they may have a hand in how those characters change. NPCs can also have fixed character development with no involvement from the player, but NPCs often change or show different parts of who they are based on the MC's development and actions. For example, in the case of *Siren Song*, Brandon turns vengeful after the death of his best friend. This is in direct response to Cecilia's actions.

For NPCs, think about their internal reactions to conflicts (whether presented by the MC or the plot at large) and their outward responses. This helps you showcase who they are in interesting ways during each of these moments and allows you to develop them as they continue to wrestle with the conflict[7] along certain branches.

Character Routes

Routes are special windows into facets of characters' lives the player doesn't see in the main story. The character route can be a significant subplot or become a main branch when the player locks into it, or it can be content that doesn't necessarily have an impact on the story as a whole, but it still provides important revelations about the character. The key is that it gives something to the player about the character that they could not have known without experiencing the character route. The character needs to develop in some way, and that development needs to be meaningful. For example, *Monster Prom*'s Damien LaVey, a literal demon from hell, is intense, threatening and intimidating, and prone to violence, which makes him giddy.

CAPTION: Damien expresses his love for fire. Screenshot from *Monster Prom*. Developed by Beautiful Glitch and protected by United States and international copyright law. © Beautiful Glitch.

However, he has a deep respect and reverence for love, due to witnessing his fathers' relationship.

CAPTION: Damien talks about his fathers and how they made love "badass." Screenshot from *Monster Prom*. Developed by Beautiful Glitch and protected by United States and international copyright law. © Beautiful Glitch.

(Continued)

At first they were despised for daring to love each other, but they showed that love made them not weaker, but stronger. And now, thanks to them, love is a badass thing down there in that circle.

CAPTION (*Continued*): Damien talks about his fathers and how they made love "badass." Screenshot from *Monster Prom*. Developed by Beautiful Glitch and protected by United States and international copyright law. © Beautiful Glitch.

Based upon Damien's behavior and dialogue for most of the game, his great respect for love will come as a shock to many players. But the scene in the event explains Damien's backstory and upbringing, makes him more respectable, and makes him a more well-rounded character.

Locking into Character Routes

When players lock into a character route, they have "[focused] on a particular character by interacting with said character over others … or by having [their] avatar[8] act in a way the player knows will appeal to the character."[9] Part of player strategy is figuring out how to lock into the character routes that interest them. This means that, to a certain degree, the game needs to telegraph to players what they should do if they're trying to develop relationships with certain NPCs and LIs. There are a myriad ways players can lock into routes, and you'll need to determine this in your branching structure's design. A common method is for players to simply choose to spend time with one character over others when presented with the option. However, there are a number of ways that players can lock into character routes. The MC's skills or skill level, items obtained, other choices made, or other good and bad relationships may be factors that attract or repel NPCs.

In *Hatoful Boyfriend*, players choose which classes and other places Hiyoko will attend during school days. Romanceable NPCs are at different locations around the school, giving players the ability to decide which pigeon boy they'd like to spend quality time with. The mechanics for locking into a route can be varied and creative and still work within the game's narrative design.

CAPTION: When players lock into a character's route, other LIs may now view the MC unfavorably. This can be because the LI is jealous; doesn't like the character whose route the player is on; or other reasons, like MC attributes. In this playthrough, the player is not on Sakuya's route, and Hiyoko's skills are high enough that she has bested Sakuya as an academic rival. Sakuya does not take kindly to this. Screenshots from *Hatoful Boyfriend*. Developed by Hato Moa, Mediatonic, and Devolver Digital and protected by United States and international copyright law. © Mediatonic.

(Continued)

CAPTION (*Continued*):   When players lock into a character's route, other LIs may now view the MC unfavorably. This can be because the LI is jealous; doesn't like the character whose route the player is on; or other reasons, like MC attributes. In this playthrough, the player is not on Sakuya's route, and Hiyoko's skills are high enough that she has bested Sakuya as an academic rival. Sakuya does not take kindly to this. Screenshots from *Hatoful Boyfriend*. Developed by Hato Moa, Mediatonic, and Devolver Digital and protected by United States and international copyright law. © Mediatonic.

PressHearttoContinue, "HATOFUL BOYFRIEND: Part 3 NAGEKI ENDING: I Promised I Wouldn't Cry …," uploaded September 13, 2014, YouTube video, 28:39, https://www.youtube.com/watch?v=KTohev37ysQ.

A stark illustration of character routes and what players might learn is *Doki Doki Literature Club!* Each of the girls' routes has a distinct plot where the MC gets to know each of the club members. The MC, who's not interested in much, gets talked into attending the school's literature club by his childhood friend. Before he joins, the club only has four members, all girls.

Locking into character routes has several steps, one of which is directly choosing to spend time alone with one of the girls during the club meetings.

CAPTION: Screenshot from *Doki Doki Literature Club Plus!* Developed by Team Salvato and protected by United States and international copyright law. © Team Salvato.
"*Doki Doki Literature Club Plus*! 100% Walkthrough Guide," SteamAH, July 1, 2021, https://steamah.com/doki-doki-literature-club-plus-100-walkthrough-guide/.

Another step is through a minigame. One way players get to know the other club members is through reading and critiquing poems the girls have written, and they spend significant amounts of time alone during these critiquing sessions. In a poetry writing minigame, the player is presented with lists of words that appeal to each of the girls based on their personalities, interests, and private issues they're struggling with in their lives. During each minigame, the MC locks into spending time sharing poems with the girl whose corresponding words the player selected the most. These words give effective characterization for these three characters, and players have to figure out which words align with which girl, based on their interactions and what they know about the girls. But these words also fore-shadow what's going on in the girls' inner worlds, and that they're keeping secret hardships from their private lives. It's these difficult, dark secrets that are slowly revealed as players progress along each character route.

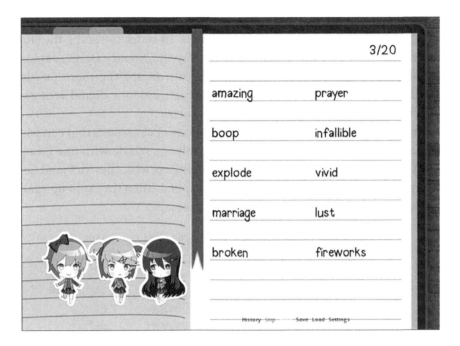

CAPTION: *Doki Doki Literature Club Plus!* poetry writing mini game. Developed by Team Salvato and protected by United States and international copyright law. © Team Salvato.
Eevee-Trainer, "Poem Word Mechanics: *Doki Doki Literature Club!*: Guide and Walkthrough (PC)," April 5, 2021, https://gamefaqs.gamespot.com/pc/222637-doki-doki-literature-club/faqs/75306/poem-word-mechanics.

Character Development along Multiple Branches

NPCs can have effective, engaging character development when they or the game don't have character-specific routes. These characters have their development within the main story and the branching structure. NPCs can have all of their development along one branch or a nested branch structure, or as the story progresses, they're developed in similar ways as an MC.

The hybrid visual novel *999: Nine Hours, Nine Persons, Nine Doors* gives individual NPCs their own stories that develop them along nested branches. Players get these stories in parts. The focus is on a couple of NPCs in one branch. The story leaves those NPCs in another branch and then returns to them later. Nine people are abducted and trapped together on a sinking luxury cruise ship. Junpei, the MC, and the other characters wake up with special LCD bracelets placed on their wrists and small bombs in their stomachs. The bracelets are numbered from 1 to 9. The ship will sink in 9 hours (sensing a theme?). In order to escape the ship before that happens, the abductees must play the Nonary Game, explore the ship, and find numbered doors, each with escape-the-room puzzles within. Only characters whose bracelets create a door's digital root can pass through that door to try and solve its puzzle.

Branching, then, is tied to the combinations of characters that can pass through the doors together. Once Junpei solves a puzzle with one group, all of the characters come back together to discuss what they've found and to try to make sense of why they were kidnapped. Then they split up again through more doors trying to find a way to escape.

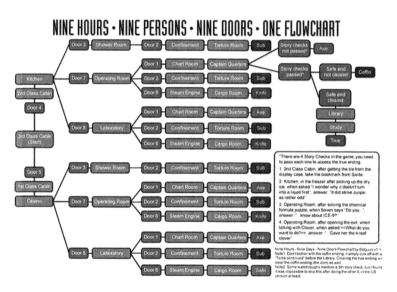

CAPTION: *999's* branching structure is based upon the doors players choose to enter.

Batguus, "*Nine Hours, Nine Persons, Nine Doors*: Room/Ending Flowchart," GameFAQs, last modified June 2, 2011, https://gamefaqs.gamespot.com/ ds/961351-nine-hours-nine-persons-nine-doors/map/7565.

Upon meeting the others, Junpei labels these characters with first impressions based on their appearances and attitudes. They become more well rounded as Junpei works with them because each character has knowledge and/or theories about their circumstances to give insight into the wider plot and why they've been forced together. Who knows what can be surprising, as subjects span math, history, science, and mysticism. Characters' abilities to share this knowledge with Junpei add a fascinating twist to who they are, and players, along with Junpei, may wonder where they've gotten that information.

How a character is introduced, when players get their backstory or history, and when players learn of their motivations are part of what make up how players perceive characters and whether they trust or like them.[10] This is true of 999's story, where each of the Nonary Game's players has some connection to the one running it. There are innocents, not-so-innocents, and villains in this group. Character development, then, is an unraveling of the mystery of each player and why they've been selected for the game.

In the case of Aoi, he plays the role of the uncooperative player who's not interested in working with the others, and he tells Junpei not to trust anyone. 999's writer, Kotaro Uchikoshi, describes Aoi as "a lone wolf … [who] self-righteously does what he wants … He often is the voice of dissent, starting arguments and causing cracks in the tenuous group peace."[11] When players select Door 4, they get to witness this side of Aoi. He fights with an older player, mocking her age with derogatory insults, and displays his sarcastic wit. Uchikoshi also hints that there is more to Aoi: "If you are able to get him to be frank, you may even be able to find out about his secret past."[12] It's only later in the game with one of the final doors that players come to understand why Aoi has a bitter outlook and prefers to be alone: he tells a sweet story about his little sister and then says she died. He blames himself.

CAPTION: Screenshot from *999*. Developed by Spike Chunsoft and protected by United States and international copyright law. © Spike Chunsoft, Co. Ltd.

Aoi's CG in this moment is a close-up of him being reflective and reliving a painful past. He's not snarky and combative—he has taken off his mask and allowed the other players to see a vulnerable side of himself. It's a well-choreographed scene that is the culmination of all of Aoi's interactions with the other abductees (and the player's impressions of the character upto this point).

Plotting the revelatory breadcrumb trail players will travel as they learn about a character (NPC or MC) can take them on an emotional journey with that character. If the plotting is done correctly, they may not end up liking the character, but the player can empathize with them and understand what life experiences have molded them into who they are.

LOVE INTERESTS (LIs)

If the game has romanceable LIs, each LI needs a character route that the player locks into. Each LI also needs at least one ending. This can be a good ending (the MC and LI are together), there can also be at least one bad ending where the MC and LI don't end up together for any number of reasons, or multiple possible endings (including secret ones) where the MC and LI wind up together in different scenarios. Each romanceable character route should feel distinct from the others, befitting the characterization of the LI. If these branches aren't balanced, the player may perceive that bias is creeping in from the writer (more on this in "Keeping Your Writing Unbiased" below). Typically, to successfully romance the LI, the player pays close attention to the LIs likes and dislikes, chooses the correct dialogue and action choices that will please the LI, and gives the LI appropriate gifts. And if the player can succeed at making the correct choices and giving the LI the right gifts, they can also *fail* in these regards. So, tracking how much an LI likes or loves the MC via variables is an important part of designing each route.

Coffee Spoon

This is where you will meet Mat when you decide to go drink coffee with Amanda.

♥ Drink choices:

Choices	Results
Godspeed You! Black Coffee	Like
Iced Teagan and Sara	Like
Chai Antwoord	Like

♥ Naming the Banana Bread:

Choices	Results
Banana Bread Kennedys	Like
Grateful (Banana) Bread	Dislike
Right Said Banana Bread	Like

The Park

This is where you will meet Brian, his daughter Daisy and his pet dog Maxwell.

♥ Meet Brian:

Choices	Results
Well, you're traditionally not supposed to aim for people's heads.	Neutral
It's a new technique.	Like
I'll catch it with my teeth next time.	Like

CAPTION: Excerpts from a walkthrough on Steam for *Dream Daddy: A Dad Dating Simulator* explain what choices the romanceable dads like, dislike, or are neutral toward. Making the choices the dads find desirable early on leads to befriending them, which leads to the player being able to romance them later.

(Continued)

Craig's Text

▼ You ready to kick some butt?:

Choices	Results
Gotta stay posi, dude.	Neutral
With your help, I am.	Like
H E L P	Dislike

CAPTION *(Continued)*:   Excerpts from a walkthrough on Steam for *Dream Daddy: A Dad Dating Simulator* explain what choices the romanceable dads like, dislike, or are neutral toward. Making the choices the dads find desirable early on leads to befriending them, which leads to the player being able to romance them later.
venus, "A Complete Guide for Dream Daddies, I Guess," Steam, last modified August 9, 2017, https://steamcommunity.com/sharedfiles/filedetails/?id=1084697185.

LI Routes

A major convention for LI routes is that they focus on what's important to romanceable characters and highlight their personalities. This differentiates the LIs from each other and keeps routes from feeling similar to players. Once players lock into the route, they may or may not be able to interact with other LIs and NPCs. Some LI routes will feature the LI exclusively, with no other characters present. In other cases, interactions between the route's LI and other characters can reveal a lot about the LI, and the player may even get some clues about nonroute LIs who appear and how to romance *them* in later playthroughs. Dating can be featured, as well, and players will have to make the right choices for a successful date. Depending on how quickly the relationship progresses, there can be one or several sex scenes along the characters' route, or the culmination of the route is an ending with a sex scene or the aftermath of the MC and LI being intimate. In mobile VNs, it is common for players to use the app's premium currency to pay for the choices that lead to sex scenes and other intimate moments with the LI.

"Hard to Get" and Difficult LIs

Another feature of VNs with multiple LIs is that at least one of these NPCs tends to be difficult to romance. With "hard to get" or otherwise difficult-to-romance LIs, assume a number of players will fail to romance them on their first or even third tries. The player has to figure out what makes these LIs difficult or hard to get. Why they're the way they are should make sense for that character. For instance, if a former partner broke the LI's heart, the LI is extremely hesitant to love again. The MC will have to gain the LI's trust through both dialogue and actions.

Robert is *Dream Daddy: A Dad Dating Simulator's* difficult LI. Upon meeting Robert in a bar, the MC can go back to Robert's place and have a one-night stand. Robert kicks the MC out of his house the next morning, and the MC sees him a little later that day at a cookout. When another LI introduces Robert to the MC, Robert is a bit standoffish, but friendly, and acts if he's not met the MC. Frustrated and wanting to reconnect, the MC DMs Robert. Robert sees the message, yet he never responds.

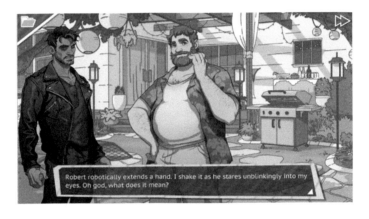

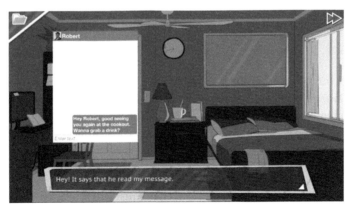

CAPTION: Robert ghosts the MC. Screenshots from *Dream Daddy: A Dad Dating Simulator.* Developed by Game Grumps and protected by United States and international copyright law. © Game Grumps.

(Continued)

CAPTION (*Continued*): Robert ghosts the MC. Screenshots from *Dream Daddy: A Dad Dating Simulator.* Developed by Game Grumps and protected by United States and international copyright law. © Game Grumps.

theshydog, "What Happens If You Sleep with Robert: *Dream Daddy*," uploaded August 3, 2017, 11:09, https://www.youtube.com/watch?v=VWbrmc7a-UM.

If players wish to romance Robert, they must learn how to do it success-fully on subsequent playthroughs if they sleep with him. Obviously, they *cannot* sleep with Robert when he invites the MC to go home with him.

Players also will learn important things about his past whether they choose to romance him or other dads.

Difficult LIs shouldn't be arbitrarily hard to romance. There should be a good reason or reasons why, which can deepen the emotional connection when the player discovers the truth. As is the case with other LIs, it should become more and more obvious how to successfully romance them the more the player learns about them. In Robert's case, he's a widower, he's estranged from his adult daughter, and he's been treated badly in a relationship he had with another of the dad LIs. He's become a loner not looking for emotional attachment for believable reasons. Knowing what the player does about him, they will still have to make the right choices based on his past and emotional hurts in order to get his good ending.

Give players clues about these LIs' personalities, interests, pasts, and emotional hang-ups through the story and interactions with them by dropping clues like bread crumbs throughout the story and their routes. Like any clues, these should be natural and arise in the context of a scene or during exploration.

KEEPING YOUR WRITING UNBIASED

I don't know a writer who thinks, *Let me make my writing biased, so I can piss off my audience.* However, players can *perceive* bias, which can take writers off guard. We're not trying to be biased! But can our bias, our preferences for certain characters over others, sink in? I was never made more aware that this is a problem for players than when I started writing and editing mobile VNs. Players get upset with choices they do and don't have in other types of games, but I don't remember seeing them call out the writing or the decisions they can make based upon the writers liking certain characters over others. I believe this is highlighted in visual novel fandoms because there's a greater intimacy between player and story, especially when players select whom they wish to romance. A secondary reason may be that they can identify the writer(s) because VNs often have one writer or a small writing team that engages with their players during crowdfunding campaigns, on social media, and in Discord servers.

> 11/18/2018
>
> I don't understand why this book has 4 LIs but don't give them decent content throughout the entire book. Half of the book was basically Vincent centered while trying to mix Allan into it. Ken was introduced first chapter but we don't have any real interactions with him until like 2/3rd of the book. Jalon had the least interactions out of everyone, we didn't even get a dedicated chapter like Ken to "make up lost time." Worst of all, Allan is the obvious popular choice but they introduced a fake rival to try and add "drama"? I know they already hinted that Allan changed when we had that shopping/cafe chapter but I felt like it was unnecessary with how it was handled in the end.

CAPTION: A player expresses displeasure with the LI routes in a mobile VN. From her point of view, the story was biased toward one LI over the other three.

I mentioned earlier in the chapter and in "Designing Branching Narratives" that making sure branches and routes are balanced can fight off perceptions of bias. Now, unconsciously or consciously, we have our favorite characters and stories as writers, and players will pick up on this. Why is this important? Why should we care? If we're writing noninteractive narratives, the audience is coming to us because they're interested in the story we have to tell them. In games, however, players want to tell their own stories, and we even have the concept of **player agency** to explain an aspect of the relationship between player and game. Player agency is the players' beliefs that their actions and choices drive what happens during their gameplay sessions and impact the game. If they believe the *writer* is the one pulling the strings, even through bias against their favorite characters, then this dilutes their agency.

Graham Reznick, who worked on *Until Dawn*, *The Dark Pictures Anthology*, and *The Quarry*, explains that players experience a "literal plot and emotional plot in all stories." The literal plot is what happens, and the emotional plot is what the player is living and "experiencing internally or interacting with" and empathizing with.[13] So, you're taking players on an emotional journey with these characters, and it is a *letdown* when they sense you're not allowing them to interact with those characters in ways that they can with others.

Techniques for Avoiding Bias

Write All Characters with the Same Care and Sincerity: Whether it has a small or large role, a*ny* character can become a favorite. You might have ideas as to why players will like every character you're creating, but someone will enjoy a character for reasons you can't foresee. Characters you don't anticipate becoming favorites do. This was certainly the case with *Siren Song*.

Give Characters of Equal Weight the Same Amount of Narrative Real Estate: By "equal weight," I mean that main characters should be treated the same as other main characters, secondary characters should be treated the same, and tertiary characters should be treated the same. Make sure that NPCs of equal weight have a similar amount of involvement in the plot. Give the MC a similar or equal number of interactions with them, and make sure their character-specific routes are balanced.

Write Your "Type's" LI Route First: If there are certain traits you find attractive in individuals, and those traits are in one of your characters, write that character's route first.[14] Use that route as a template for the others by having a similar or equal number of emotional beats, dates, revelatory moments, etc.

Of course, taking care to try to eliminate any bias players might perceive *does not* mean they won't think you're biased. But attempts to keep bias out of the writing can only make for better stories because you're mindful of and refining character details, characterization, and development.

EXERCISES

1. Choice Points as Characterization

    Design a choice point that diverges into a couple of branches. Each branch should illustrate a different aspect of the MC's personality.

    - Include choices along each branch that will cause conflict between the MC and at least one NPC.

2. Character Routes

    Design a character route for an NPC, LI or non-LI. Create a plot scenario focused on the NPC that progresses along the route.

    - Decide where along the route players will get small and large revelations about the character.

    - Add emotional beats that either strengthen or weaken the character's relationships to the MC or other NPCs.

NOTES

1 A character archetype is one that frequently shows up in all types of storytelling media. No matter the story, these characters have similarities to other characters of the same archetype. They have a particular personality, background, pattern of behavior, role in the plot, and/or role in relationships.

2 The second-most important character after the protagonist.

3 Chloe Spencer, "If You Like *The Grudge*, You Might Like This Visual Novel," Kotaku, August 18, 2017, https://kotaku.com/if-you-liked-the-grudge-you-might-like-this-visual-nov-1797972825.

4 More so than romancing these characters, the players' goal is to increase the right stats so that the dateable characters will find them interesting/ desirable enough to accept an invitation to prom. That means that a player may not choose to spend time with a particular monster or try to romance them, and they can *still* successfully invite that monster to prom!

5 Michelle Clough, message to author, April 25, 2022.

6 Graham Reznick, Sam Maggs, Karin Weekes, Sam Barlow, and Christian Divine, "Developing Branching Narratives: LudoNarraCon 2020 Panel, April 25, 2020," YouTube video, 48:05, https://www.youtube.com/watch?v=mgD81pQlu1o.

7 A conflict should not be viewed as something that is inherently negative. Conflicts, like consequences, can be positive or negative. For example, internal and external conflicts confronting an MC or NPC challenge them to become a better person because of their circumstances or the people around them.

8 The MC or player-character.

9 David Neri, "Reflections on the Computer Screen: An Examination of Western/Horror Visual Novels' Commentary on Traditional Eastern VN Romance Tropes," *ReVisions*, (2018): 8.

10 Your end goal can certainly be players *not* trusting or liking characters!

11 Chris Hoffman, "9 Reasons to Love 999: The Novel for iOS," MacLife, March 10, 2014, https://web.archive.org/web/20140618141919/http://www.maclife.com/article/games/9_reasons_love_999_novel_ios.

12 Ibid.

13 Graham Reznick, Sam Maggs, Karin Weekes, Sam Barlow, and Christian Divine, "Developing Branching Narratives: LudoNarraCon 2020 Panel," April 25, 2020, YouTube video, 48:05, https://www.youtube.com/watch?v=mgD81pQlu1o.

14 Michelle Clough, message to author, April 14, 2022.

CHAPTER 10

Dialogue in Visual Novels and Choice-Based Games

Choose Your Words Carefully

C HOICES LEADING TO MULTIPLE branching routes are a hallmark of the storytelling in visual novels. Another is its dialogue. As in any story, dialogue is a vehicle of characterization for both protagonists and other characters. One of the crucial ways players get information is through dialogue and dialogue trees. Dialogue is part of the main story, but it also gives players the opportunity to get to know non-player characters (NPCs) that interest them (romantically and platonically). This chapter won't focus on the technical aspects of coding dialogue or reviewing the best engines for branching dialogue (there are a number of questions to think about in choosing the right tools). Here, we're addressing designing the experience players will have in interacting with characters through what they say.

DOI: 10.1201/9781003199724-12

DIALOGUE IS *ALWAYS* FUNCTIONAL

When writers discuss dialogue, they tend to focus on the creative aspect of what characters say, not the functional reasons for *why* they say it. Dialogue will always have a functional role in any scene, whether the story is prose fiction, a film, a comic, or a game. The dialogue is always doing something specific, and it's communicating something to the audience beyond the words coming out of the characters' mouths.

Dialogue in games has both functions of narrative design and functions of game writing or story.

Narrative Design's Dialogue Functions[1]

Guide Players through a Tutorial: At the beginning of a game (and at specific points), a character explains controls, skills, abilities, etc., to players and tells them why these mechanics and controls are important.

Give Mission Objectives: A character tells players exactly what they need to do to successfully complete a mission or quest.

Introduce a New Mechanic: The game teaches players a new mechanic and how it works.

Explain a New Skill: The game teaches players a new skill and how it works.

Game Writing/Story's Dialogue Functions[2]

Progress the Story via Choices: When players make a dialogue choice, they're deciding how the story will branch and how those branches will reconnect with the main story.

Present Background Information or Lore: Characters may say something about past events or give worldbuilding insights.

Convey Character Development: Speaking characters, including the player-character/main characters (MC), may express their own character development, or characters may indicate they've noticed changes in a specific character.

Express Characterization: How characters speak (their accents/verbal tics, whether they use slang or "high-falutin" elevated language; their diction) and what they choose to talk about illustrates aspects of the characters' personalities and what's important to them.

Introduce a Plot Point and/or Foreshadow Future Plot Points: Characters may drop a subtle or not-so-subtle hint about something that happens later.

You can use any of these functions in visual novels, especially if they have a variety of mechanics or skills/abilities MCs can acquire. As you're writing dialogue, keep its function(s) in mind. One line of dialogue can have multiple roles. The nature of branching dialogue highlights these roles.

DIALOGUE CHOICES AND DIALOGUE TREES

An essential tool players use to express whom they believe the MC to be is through dialogue choices. Through certain dialogue choices, the MC illustrates different aspects of their personality. The player can decide what kind of character they want their MC to be because, as Sam Maggs puts it so well, "there's no correct version of that person."[3]

Dialogue Choices and the MC's Personality

However you display parts of the MC's personality through dialogue choices, those choices *must always* be within character. A character can say something outrageous or choose to do something unexpected, but it is still a part of their make-up.

Imagine an MC who appears poised and confident to everyone she meets, and she seems to attack every goal or problem with that same level of confidence. She's also aware that everyone sees her that way. But she's actually intimidated by anyone she believes is more intelligent than she is. These aspects of her personality should come out in some of her dialogue choices and with specific characters.

So, if she's trying to solve who stole her watch, she might address a co-worker next to her cubicle with these questions:

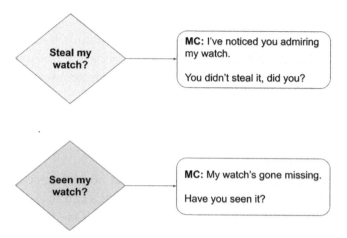

CAPTION: Image made in Google Slides. © Toiya Kristen Finley.

The MC is confident and poised. She's direct in both questions, whether she accuses her co-worker of stealing the watch or asks if he's seen it.

The MC has the same goal of reclaiming her watch when she questions a co-worker from a department down the hall. She's watched this co-worker handle difficult clients, which blew her away. The MC is a little bit afraid of her.

This time, she's not as confident, and she's a little nervous and deferential toward this co-worker because the MC is intimidated.

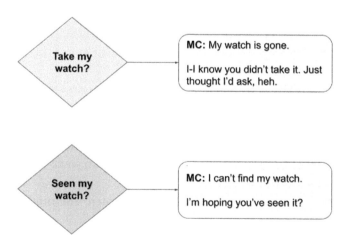

CAPTION: Image made in Google Slides. © Toiya Kristen Finley.

So, the goal is the same in each conversation (find who stole the watch), but how the MC addresses these NPCs is different, based on her personality and how she views them.

MC Character Development and Characterization

Players develop their characters and define their characterization through a morality system (or karma system) in some popular games. *Fable*, the *Red Dead Redemption* franchise, and *Undertale* all have morality systems that keep track of the number of "good" and "bad" choices players make, and in the *Mass Effect* franchise, Shepard can be a paragon or a renegade. But a game does not have to have a morality system to have choices based on grey or less grey choices. For example, players have the option to lie or tell the truth. They might be able to alleviate another character's pain by offering them medicine (or not) or give water to someone who's dehydrated (or not). The decisions players make in these moments will have at least one immediate consequence, and the choice will probably have a later influence on the story.

These types of choices that fall along the moral spectrum give players more freedom to define who the MC is and who they're becoming. Do they want a character who always "does the right thing"? A character who always tries to get along with everybody? A character who is amoral and relishes in misdeeds? One who doesn't mind being a jerk to get what they want? Or a character who is complicated and sports all shades of moral greys?

Just as the MC/player-character's dialogue choices must be in character, characters also need to respond and react in character, and sometimes illustrate how they view the MC, which lends further characterization to the MC. In the stolen watch example, the co-worker in the cubicle next to the MC keeps his head down and tries to stay out of trouble. He doesn't know the MC very well.

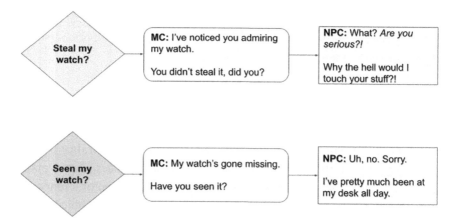

CAPTION: Image made in Google Slides. © Toiya Kristen Finley.

As he's accused by the MC that he has stolen her watch, the co-worker is both shocked and takes it as an affront. He intentionally doesn't bother her or anyone else, so why would she think poorly of him? With the other dialogue choice, he makes it clear that he stays focused on his work.

The co-worker from the department down the hall is pretty confident like the MC, but she has a sense of humor about things and doesn't get involved with petty office politics or let them affect her job.

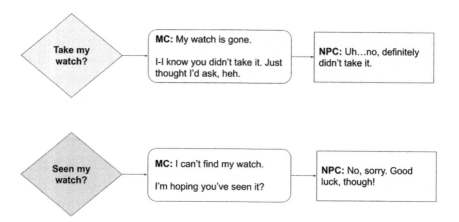

CAPTION: Image made in Google Slides. © Toiya Kristen Finley.

The MC tries to avoid being confrontational when saying she knows her co-worker didn't take the watch, but she has to ask anyway. The co-worker is weirded out by this, but she doesn't take it personally (or at least she doesn't let the MC know if she does). With the other option, the co-worker wishes the MC luck because it's in her nature to maintain decent relationships with those she works with, even if they're acquaintances.

Both co-workers have very different reactions based on their own personalities and the personality of the MC.

Players can use dialogue choices strategically to alter relationships. Dialogue choices allow them to express how they feel about relationships and give them control over how they want those relationships to progress. They can be intentionally mean or say something they know a character won't like. They can use these choices strategically to keep themselves from locking into a character route or to make sure they don't spend more time with someone they don't like or have no interest in. Or, if they like a character or want to romance an LI, they can pick all of the dialogue choices that will emphasize the parts of the MC's personality the character finds most attractive or worthwhile.

NPC Character Development

Conversations are great ways for NPCs to get their own character development. Players spend time with them and get to know them better. What players choose to say to them slowly reveals certain things about them. In the way some branches are designed, players need to figure out the correct dialogue choices to unlock secrets on a character's route, or they might have to play a character's route several times or go through a dialogue tree a couple of times to learn all of the information about the NPC contained within them.

In *Hatoful Boyfriend*, Nageki has a realization about himself during his route. He's trapped in the library. During any attempts to leave, Nageki ends up losing consciousness and waking up in the library. Hiyoko is the only one who visits him. Nageki had believed he was being bullied by the other students because he thought they were ignoring him. But, in spending time with Hiyoko, he slowly regains his memory and sense of who he is … and was. He's a ghost who died in the library, and that's why he can't leave.

CAPTION: During Hiyoko and Nageki's conversation, Nageki asks Hiyoko why no one else talks to him. Developed by Hato Moa, Mediatonic, and Devolver Digital and protected by United States and international copyright law. © Mediatonic.

PressHearttoContinue, "HATOFUL BOYFRIEND: Part 3 NAGEKI ENDING: I Promised I Wouldn't Cry …," uploaded September 13, 2014, YouTube video, 28:39, https://www.youtube.com/watch?v=KTohev37ysQ.

There is an important caveat to NPC character development; sometimes, the focus shifts from the MC as the driver of the story, and the NPC becomes the star of a scene.[4] But it is the player's story, told through the MC, so even character routes need to have the player-character at their heart. In the case of Nageki, he is only able to remember who he is and the tragic way in which he died because of Hiyoko's kindness and friendship toward him. She's patient with him, gives him the space to sometimes be annoyed with her when she's too loud in the library, and encourages him to share.

Dialogue Trees

Players will read or listen to dialogue in scenes, but they also have the power to control interactions with characters or decide how the story will progress through choices during conversations. These conversations, called dialogue trees, are between the MC and one or more NPCs. Dialogue trees are a tool of player agency and character customization because "[p]layers tend to feel more attached to and interested in the game's protagonist"[5] when they're expressing who the MC is and determining how the MC will proceed through the story. These trees branch and have multiple choice points leading to nested branches. The steps of a dialogue tree proceed a little something like this:

1. NPC addresses the MC.

2. Player chooses the MC's response. This can be dialogue or an action.

3. NPC reacts based on the MC's response.

4. MC reacts to the NPC's reaction.

5. The conversation ends (with shorter trees), or the NPC has another reaction, leading to a new set of choices.

The player is trying to find out who's started a nasty rumor about them in the following dialogue tree.

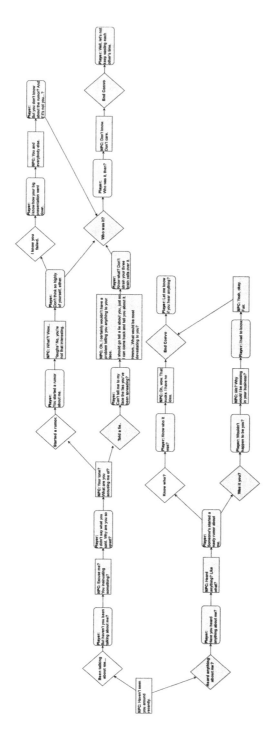

CAPTION: Dialogue chart made in draw.io. © Toiya Kristen Finley.

In the dialogue tree where the player confronts the NPC about the rumor, the player can take two tactics to establish the tone of the conversation after the NPC greets them with "Haven't seen you around recently." On one hand, the player can insinuate that the NPC is the one who has spread the rumor ("But haven't you been talking about me?"), causing a confrontation where the player and NPC end up insulting each other. In one of those nested branches, the NPC tells the player "… you're not that interesting." And in the other nested branch, the NPC threatens to come up with a lie to devastate the player. The player, in turn, will insult the NPC's intelligence ("Don't strain your three brain cells over it") or have the opportunity to share the NPC's failure ("I know how your big presentation went down"), depending on the nested branch.

With the other dialogue choice at the start of the conversation, the player is more diplomatic ("Have you heard anything about me?"). The player can later directly ask if it's the NPC who's spread the rumor in this branch, but the tone is less accusatory to begin with, so the question isn't as confrontational: "Wouldn't happen to be you?" The NPC is still taken aback, but he doesn't get angry: "*Me?* Why would I be messing in your business?"

A feature of a lot of dialogue trees is that they allow players to return to choices they didn't pick the first time, or the player can choose to end the conversation once they've progressed through all of the branches or gotten the information in which they were interested. Players can "opt in and out of certain information" and "investigate and return to topics in lesser and greater detail."[6] In some cases, depending on the NPC, what the MC says or does during the conversation, and the relationship between the two, the NPC can cut off the conversation and refuse to keep speaking to the MC. Or the dialogue choices available will be slightly different based on whether the relationship is positive, negative, or neutral.

Keep in mind that how complex your dialogue trees will be requires the same considerations as the plot's branching structures. More branching means broader scopes, more assets, longer production times, more working hours, and higher budgets.

WRITING AND PRESENTING DIALOGUE

While dialogue has technical, gameplay-related and creative, story-related functions, it still needs to be written in character and for an audience that will hear it (if it's voiced) or read it (if it's unvoiced). Visual novels have some additional conventions involving text and the presentation of dialogue. You also should take into account how dialogue is presented and the way it *looks*.

Voiced vs. Unvoiced

Visual novels[7] are thought of as games that are read, so the fact that some have at least a partial number of their lines voiced sometimes gets overlooked. Voiced and unvoiced lines should not be written in the same way. Because a voice actor performs voiced lines, you don't want to write them in a way that makes them difficult to read. While you may use these in moderation, when you write lines stringing together assonance,[8] consonance,[9] alliteration,[10] verbal/vocal tics,[11] and flowery/ornate language,[12] these can trip up the actor's tongue and sound unnatural to the player. Eye dialect[13] can make the character sound too caricatured or uneducated, even if the writing is an accurate representation of the accent phonetically.

Also, a benefit of having voice actors perform dialogue is that they can express the characters' personalities through accents (therefore, no need for eye dialect) and inflections to express how grandiose or silly a character comes across (cutting down the need for stylistic choices like assonance, consonance, and lots of flowery language).

And while you might include a sprinkling of made-up words here and there from lore, you'll also want to avoid overdoing it. This can sound preposterous and garbled, and it can confuse players who can't put all of those made-up words into context.

However, alliteration, assonance, consonance, flowery language, and preposterous-sounding lore work in *text-based* and unvoiced dialogue. These make the writing more interesting and amusing, and they work with the overall tone of the story. This kind of language creates an overall atmosphere and mood, as well. Over-the-top language is especially good when the game or the character is over the top.

VOICED EMOTES AND CATCHPHRASES

Voiced emotes are short and expressive. They tend to be laughter, sighs, groans, "hmmm," and "oh" (both sad "oh" and surprised "oh"). Each character will have their own emotes, which allows players to have some idea of what characters' voices sound like and to get a better feel for their personalities. The emote usually triggers (or plays) at the same time as a line of unvoiced dialogue. The emote gives some additional emotional context to the line.

Characters will also have their own catchphrases, which serve the same function as emotes. Sometimes, there's not a direct emotional fit between the catchphrase and the line it accompanies, but the catchphrase gives a more general mood for the character. For example, *Dream Daddy's* Hugo will exclaim "Sweet manchego!" to express pleasure or surprise.

Since there's no voice actor to express the character's personality, accent, or verbal tics, the writing needs to do this instead. A word or two written in eye dialect help players "hear" the accent the eye dialect represents, but you don't want to overdo it in text-based dialogue, either. It can be hard and annoying to read.

Writing Visual Dialogue

We easily forget that text is visual. Players have to look at it in order to read it. There's a lot of things we can imply by the way the text simply looks.[14]

This font's personality is different than

this font's personality.

And this font's personality is different than

this font's personality.

CAPTION: Image made in Google Slides. © Toiya Kristen Finley.

You can develop a visual style, and players will quickly figure out that when characters speak words in red, they're angry; when the text box has icicles hanging off of it, the character is being emotionally cold toward the addressee; etc. You can use text to convey a lot of things:

Characteristics and Personalities: What characters say (word choice) reveals their characterization. A character who greets you with "How ya doin'?" would probably not say, "Well, how auspicious to see you, darling."

Accents/Dialects: Some words spelled phonetically (eye dialect) to mimic an accent or dialect can tell players where that character is from.

Mood: The way in which you present and/or spell words can tell players about a character's mood or physical state: "I'm so *tiiirrrrred*" or "I'd suggest you NOT talk to me right now!"

Sarcasm: Italics or all caps, in context, make a character come across as sarcastic: "Oh, how *thoughtful* of you! I never would have figured it out myself."

Location: Dialogue can be directional in that it suggests how close to or far away from each other characters are. Since the MC is often a stand-in for the player, this dialogue can convey to players where the speaking character is. A line like "Hey! Come over here!" serves two purposes: (1) it tells the player the speaking character isn't close, and (2) it suggests that the MC/player-character moves closer to the character without having to show or narrate it.

Onomatopoeia: Onomatopoeic words convey nonverbalizations and help the player hear these utterances:

- *Sigh*

- GAG

- Tee hee!

Emphasis: All caps, bolding, asterisks, and italics suggest where characters are placing *emphasis* as they speak, whether they're SHOUTING or RAISING THEIR VOICES or **highlighting** something.

CAPTION: Makoto's onomatopoeic exclamation as he realizes the reality of the situation. Screenshot from *Danganronpa: Trigger Happy Havoc*. Developed by Spike Chunsoft and protected by United States and international copyright law. © Spike Chunsoft, Co. Ltd.

Lacry, "*Danganronpa: Trigger Happy Havoc* Full Walkthrough Gameplay: No Commentary (PC Longplay)," February 21, 2021, YouTube video, 1:00:56:07, https://www.youtube.com/watch?v=h88iXwonb_E.

When you're working with the team (or if the team is you), talk about the fonts you're going to use and discuss how you want to convey textual tricks (like emphasis or onomatopoeia). Some font sets may not include bold or italics.

Think about all of the ways you might express characters' personalities and emotional states through the *visuals* of text.

Dialogue and Portraits

MC and NPC portraits (headshots of the characters or images of them from the shoulders up) commonly appear in or next to the dialogue text box on the left or right. The benefit of having the portrait is that it is a visual that can match the mood or emotion characters intimate in their dialogue. Because portraits are often used when the MC is speaking but not onscreen, they allow you to show the MC's reaction to NPCs or the situation.

Characters can have multiple portraits expressing a range of emotions like happy, serious, gleeful, annoyed, angry, etc. Choosing the right emotion in the character portrait will not only match the emotional tone of the dialogue, but it will also give players a visual of the emotion on the character's face, making that emotion more palpable.

CAPTION: empressarcana, "My OTP might be AshBella but I have definitely considered many and I do mean *many* pairing combinations for the characters in *The Letter*. Rare ships including and not limited to ...," Tumblr, September 13, 2017, https://yangyangmobile.tumblr.com/post/165280308499/me-is-interested-in-knowing-what-a-lukebella. Developed by Yangyang Mobile and protected by United States and international copyright law. © Yangyang Mobile.

CAPTION: "*The Letter*," The Visual Novel Database, accessed May 8, 2022, https://vndb.org/v18550. Developed by Yangyang Mobile and protected by United States and international copyright law. © Yangyang Mobile.

In these two scenes from *The Letter*, Luke is offscreen and has two very different reactions. Notice how the emotional states in his portraits pair up with the meaning and tone of his dialogue. Giving the dialogue a stronger emotional context by matching the MC's dialogue with a portrait is especially useful when the MC is not onscreen.

Dialogue and Color

Story-heavy games focused on characters, not just visual novels (VNs), color code characters' dialogue. Every speaking character's dialogue is in a specific color. This is mostly an aesthetic choice that associates certain colors with characters. In Telltale's *The Walking Dead* series, Kenny's dialogue is a shade of green. At the end of the first season, his whereabouts are unknown. Clementine and Kenny are reunited in episode two of the second season. Before Kenny's revealed onscreen, players hear his voice and see his dialogue. Some players identified the shade of the green dialogue as belonging to Kenny before recognizing the familiar sound of Kenny's voice actor. Dialogue in specific colors is another way to differentiate characters and give text some visual appeal. If you're going to give characters their own unique color for dialogue, keep colorblind players in mind. The more characters there are, the more shades you'll have to start using.

Dialogue and Emphasizing Information

Color coding or bolding key words and phrases in dialogue (and other text) is another VN convention. Color coding makes those words and phrases stand out and draws players' eyes to them. Often, the color coding is for information players would do well to remember or think about, or it points out useful items or objects players can add to their inventory or details about those objects.

CAPTION: "They," the killer, is emphasized using asterisks, and the key informational phrase is bolded in yellow. Screenshot from *Danganronpa: Trigger Happy Havoc Anniversary Edition*. Developed by Spike Chunsoft and protected by United States and international copyright law. © Spike Chunsoft, Co. Ltd. Justonegamr, "Chapter 1 Class Trial Playthrough: *Danganronpa: Trigger Happy Havoc Anniversary Edition* [iOS]," May 21, 2020, YouTube video, 1:32:24, https://www.youtube.com/watch?v=jYD0ZGaeqU0.

Beyond giving players important information the game doesn't want them to miss, color coding and/or bolding words is a playful way to interact with players and give the text more visual interest.

Dialogue and Text Boxes

One thing you want to determine early on in your user interface (UI) design process is how many maximum characters (letters, spaces, and punctuation—not just words) a text box can fit comfortably without the words and lines looking cramped. This goes for any type of text box in the game, including choice text boxes. If you have already written your script, you can plug your lines in to the text boxes to see how they fit. Depending on what you and your UI designer decide, you may have to go back and revise your script so that the text looks good. Therefore, determining the minimums and maximums for characters in text boxes is something you want to do sooner rather than later.

Text boxes contain dialogue, but there are ways they also can convey extra information about the nature of the dialogue or the character speaking it. A very familiar VN convention is "???." Dialogue text boxes include the name of the speaking character. However, when characters are introduced and neither the MC nor the player know their names, the name of the character will appear as "???," since it would not make sense for the name to appear before the player knows it.

CAPTION: The "???" convention used in *Hatoful Boyfriend*. The speaking character is offscreen and has not been introduced. Developed by Hato Moa, Mediatonic, and Devolver Digital and protected by United States and international copyright law. © Mediatonic.
PressHearttoContinue, "*HATOFUL BOYFRIEND*: Part 1: Our first day of school ...," YouTube, uploaded September 11, 2014, https://www.youtube.com/watch?v=3QHYdHfIiUo.

The *shape* of a dialogue text box aids in communicating tone, personality, and whether a character is thinking or speaking. Thanks to a history of comics and manga, text boxes already have an established visual language from speech balloons. You can use that knowledge players already have from comics and manga to your advantage.

Meanings of Dialogue Text Box Shapes[15]

Jagged: Screaming or shouting.

Icy (with Hanging Icicles): Hostility toward the addressee.

Rough: Monstrous, sinister (good for creatures, too).

Electronic: Robotic or indicating transmission over electronic devices.

Wavy: Drunk or high.

CAPTION: A mockup of a dialogue text box asset emulating the terror and sadness the MC, Vincent, feels in the moment. UI design by Jules Riseling. Developed by Schnoodle Studio and protected by United States and international copyright law. © Schnoodle Studio.

In some final thoughts on dialogue, I want to address the length of the lines themselves. As I said before, VN players expect to read. They like reading VNs. However, we need to consider the type of visual novel when deciding how long lines of text should be. Mobile games are made for short attention spans. Most players spend 4–6 minutes in their mobile sessions.[16] Meaning they don't have a lot of time to read. Therefore, mobile VN dialogue should be shorter and succinct. But sometimes it also needs to be a little on the nose, so players don't miss key information.[17] Players have a tendency to simply tap through (skip) text on the smartphone screen. Having strict character counts will be beneficial here because the restrictions will force you to keep your dialogue short and to the point.

But that doesn't mean that dialogue for nonmobile VNs can be long and rambling. Just because you have the space doesn't mean you have to use it. A rambling monologue or two might make sense for certain characters, but if characters are engaged in conversation, one of them isn't likely to hijack the conversation with long lines of dialogue.

However long or short your lines of dialogue are, make sure that they always have a function and that they remain in character.

EXERCISE

Design a dialogue tree with one NPC. You can write it out on paper; prototype it in tools like Twine or ink; or diagram it using a flowchart tool, like Lucidchart, draw.io, or Google Drawings—whatever method makes the most sense so that you can easily visualize your design.

What is the scenario for this dialogue tree's conversation? Why is the MC talking to the character? What types of information might the player glean from this conversation?

In the dialogue tree's branches,

- give each line of dialogue a specific function;

- show off different aspects of the MC's and NPC's personalities;

- find ways to communicate tone to the player;

- consider using onomatopoeia, italics, and bolding; and

- give the player the option to leave the conversation without exhausting all questions in a branch.

NOTES

1 Adapted from Toiya Kristen Finley, *Narrative Tactics for Mobile and Social Games: Pocket-Sized Storytelling* (Boca Raton, FL: CRC Press, 2019), 96–97.
2 Ibid.
3 Graham Reznick, Sam Maggs, Karin Weekes, Sam Barlow, and Christian Divine, "Developing Branching Narratives: LudoNarraCon 2020 Panel," April 25, 2020, YouTube video, 48:05, https://www.youtube.com/watch?v=mgD8lpQlulo.
4 Alexander Freed, "Branching Conversation Systems and the Working Writer, Part 4: Key Principles," Game Developer, September 24, 2014, https://www.gamedeveloper.com/design/branching-conversation-systems-and-the-working-writer-part-4-key-principles.
5 Alexander Freed, "Branching Conversation Systems and the Working Writer, Part 1: Introduction," Game Developer, September 2, 2014, https://www.gamedeveloper.com/design/branching-conversation-systems-and-the-working-writer-part-1-introduction.

6 Carrie Patel, "Carrie Patel: Fundamentals of Branching Dialogue (SGDA Summit 2018)," uploaded May 16, 2018, YouTube video, 1:01:52, https://www.youtube.com/watch?v=Q7-QTCTlTY8.

7 Adapted from Toiya Kristen Finley, *Narrative Tactics for Mobile and Social Games: Pocket-Sized Storytelling* (Boca Raton, FL: CRC Press, 2019), 105–106.

8 The repetition of the same vowel sounds in adjacent words starting with different consonants: "The rain in Spain …"

9 The repetition of consonant sounds: "Keeping perfect pitch takes discipline."

10 The repetition of consonant sounds at the beginning of a series of words: "Stop sticking steaks on the steel stove."

11 A vocalization or word an individual utters with frequency (sometimes to show nerves or anxiety). *The Lord of the Rings's* Gollum has several verbal tics, including "precious."

12 Any combination of assonance, consonance, alliteration, made-up words, etc.: "The gauche and grotesque Manrey has the *audacity* to bribe the majestic magistrate of Blytheheight!"

13 Misspellings to phonetically represent accents and dialect: "Heya! Watcha doin'?"

14 Adapted from Toiya Kristen Finley, *Narrative Tactics for Mobile and Social Games: Pocket-Sized Storytelling* (Boca Raton, FL: CRC Press, 2019), 107–108.

15 Ibid.

16 Mihovil Grguric, "Mobile Game Session Length: How to Track & Increase It," *Udonis* (blog), January 3, 2022, https://www.blog.udonis.co/mobile-marketing/mobile-games/session-length.

17 Carrie Patel, "Carrie Patel: Fundamentals of Branching Dialogue (SGDA Summit 2018)," uploaded May 16, 2018, YouTube video, 1:01:52, https://www.youtube.com/watch?v=Q7-QTCTlTY8.

CHAPTER 11

Writing for VN and Other Choice-Based Apps

W ITH STUDIOS LIKE PIXELBERRY (Choices) and Crazy Maple Studio (Chapters) hiring freelancers to write visual novels for their apps, you're going to have opportunities to work with established and newer developers of interactive fiction. You may be responsible for developing new intellectual property (IP) (a completely new story), or you might be writing within an established universe. These developers usually have multiple series set within universes they've designed. However, you won't need to be well versed in these universes. Your client will most likely give you plenty of documents like bibles, character bios, summaries/breakdowns, and outlines to ground you in the universe. If some of the stories in the series have been published, you'll want to play them to get a sense of the world, characters, and overall tones.

Every developer will have a different production and workflow process for writers. Understanding these processes will make it easier for you to

DOI: 10.1201/9781003199724-13

understand your responsibilities and will make your onboarding go more smoothly. While developers have different production and implementation workflows, you will most likely find yourself in one of three scenarios as a freelancer:

- You will be responsible for drafting a detailed outline, creating characters and writing their bios/descriptions, and possibly creating locations.

- You will work with a detailed outline and characters developed by the client.

- You will be given general notes for the story and/or characters, and you will be responsible for developing them into a detailed outline.

How might you handle each of these scenarios?

WHEN YOU WRITE THE OUTLINE

Sometimes, the developer will give you a template or example outline for you to use. In other situations, the client won't have a formatting standard for the outline. This means you will need to figure out the best way to format your outlines so that they're easy to read by the narrative/editing team and other teams who will be responsible for implementing the story's text, art, animation, and sound assets.

In general, your outline will need to break down information about chapters/episodes,[1] choices, and premium summaries.

Provide Chapter Summaries: Each chapter summary should explain the plot for the chapter, mention the characters who will be featured in that chapter, and note the location(s) in which the chapter will be situated. These can be short paragraphs or bullet points. Whoever reads these summaries should be able to see how each chapter will transition into the next, how you're handling character development for multiple characters, and how you're designing the main plot and subplots.

Provide Choice Summaries: Detail where each chapter will branch into choices and give a sense of what these choices will be. Also, summarize what the results of these choices will be. Will they affect the plot? Will they change the player's relationship to characters, etc.?

You can include the choices in the chapter paragraph summaries, or you can add notes on what the choices will be in bullet points after each chapter summary.

Summarize Premium Choices: Indicate which choices are meant to be premium choices. These will give players access to special content. Note whether that content will be a special scene or dialogue or something like a skin that the player can wear in the story. If the premium content will gain more favorable responses or interactions from non-player characters (NPCs), be sure to explain this and how premium choices will affect the story. (Please see below for more on premium content.)

WORKING FROM AN EXISTING OUTLINE

Some developers have their visual novels' structures down to an exact science. Using analytics, Episode Interactive (Episode: Choose Your Story) can determine where players quit reading. These data also dictate how long episodes should be and what story genres players prefer.[2]

You might work off a template. The structure for each script will be given to you. These can be simple or complex. Every plot point may be given to you in the template (detailed plot points, relationship arcs, and story structure for each chapter/episode), and you will be given exact information, like how many words each scene (including premium scenes) need to be. Or the instructions may be in more broad strokes, like a brief summary of each chapter or episode. Other developers may tell you more general information, like "The MC needs to meet the first LI by Chapter 2" or "The main character (MC) needs to face a major conflict by the end of Episode 1."

Information You May Need to Fill Into the Template

- **Time of Day:** Scenes may take place in the morning, afternoon, or night. Choosing the time of day will signal to the art team to choose background assets that correspond with the correct time of day.

- **Premium, Secret, or Hidden Content:** There may be a formula to determine where premium or other special content will fall in every chapter or after a certain number of chapters. Summarize what this content will be.

- **Major Plot Points per Chapter/Episode:** Indicate where the MC will meet LIs or other important NPCs, conflicts, and other plot points that will have dramatic impact on the story.

FLESHING OUT AN EXISTING OUTLINE

Some developers will give you more freedom to create the create the VN's plot and characters. This is especially true when they've commissioned you to write new games, and you design everything about the story. When it's your responsibility to flesh out an existing outline, there's some critical information you'll want to include so that your client or an employer understands your vision and can design assets for the game.

Information to Include in a Detailed Outline

- **Minimum/Maximum Words per Scene or Chapter Summaries:** The developer may give you word restrictions for your summaries. Adhere to them! Don't write more or less than what's asked of you. Sometimes, you may be asked to write the outline before you're formally hired to write the game. Following these instructions is part of the test.

- **Number of Arcs:** Developers publish VNs of different lengths. Some of their games may be 10 chapters, while others are 15, 20, or 25 chapters. Explain how many arcs the VN will have and where chapters will fall: **Arc 1**: Chapters 1–5, **Arc 2**: Chapters 6–10, for example.

- **Total Number of Scenes per Episode/Chapter:** Every scene needs specific assets to stage it, from the MC and NPC sprites, to the background environments and music. Knowing how many scenes will be in a chapter helps with planning. This also provides the story flow at a glance, and you might get feedback that the story is moving too quickly or slowly, and you need to add or remove some scenes.

- **Number of Choices per Scene or Chapter/Episode:** You may be instructed to have a certain minimum and maximum number of choices. So, you want to explain just how many choices there will be in each scene or chapter/episode.

- **Assets to Use in Each Scene (more on this later in the chapter):** The developer may already have premade assets. You will choose from these to help stage scenes. Or you may need to design assets for your game.

- **Premium Content Summaries:** Note which choices are premium, which scenes are unlocked via premium choices, and if the player will earn any special skins or other virtual goods for unlocking premium content.

DESIGNING CHARACTERS AND LOCATIONS

If you're working within an established series, you'll probably have character and location assets chosen for you, or you will pick premade assets to stage scenes. When those assets don't already exist, it may be your responsibility to help design them. Write brief descriptions for characters and locations in your story. These don't have to be super detailed. Artists need to know how you visualize characters, their ages, and what their personalities are like. They don't usually ask for background information and histories, unless you'll be writing a series, or you're helping to create a series that you and other writers will work on. Your information for background art (locations) might simply be what the location is, what times of day the story will take place there, and some visual references. There's no need to go into a lot of worldbuilding, unless, again, you're creating a series, and the detailed documentation will serve as a reference for several games. Whether you're designing characters or locations, artist references are great at communicating your ideas, so you'll want to choose them purposefully.

DESIGNING PREMIUM CONTENT

Premium content is a huge part of mobile VNs and other types of mobile games, and players unlock it through microtransactions or the game's special currency, which players can collect after a certain period of time every day. Because players use in-game premium currency or pay for premium content, it needs to feel special when players experience it. In other words, players need to feel like the premium content is *worth* it. It needs to be differentiated from the "regular" story. Mobile VNs can have several types of premium content.

Types of Premium Content

Premium content is largely determined by the game's genre. Most VNs on mobile are romance, so premium content offers players opportunities to interact in more intimate scenes (or even love scenes) with their preferred LIs, or they might choose to spend some extra time with characters they like. However, there are all sorts of ways to incorporate premium content so that it feels like a natural part of the story.

Unlocked Love Scenes/Other Scenes. As mentioned above, players can pay for intimate scenes with their MC and LIs. These are usually unlocked when players use the premium in-game currency to pay for a choice. That choice will then automatically improve the relationship with an LI or other NPC the player wants to impress.

The premium choice can also lead directly to a love or sex scene. These scenes tend to be longer than other scenes in the game, and they should be, considering that the player is paying for them.

The experience in these scenes should also be markedly different than scenes stemming from nonpremium choices. A nonpremium choice might lead to a scene where the LI kisses the back of the MC's hand or says something loving to them, but it is much less intimate than the premium scene.

These scenes don't have to be love scenes. They might be extended moments, longer scenes than nonpremium ones. These are opportunities to show characters in a different light, to let players see another side of them. Since *Siren Song* is a humorous horror game, I included where one of the main characters' adversaries, Ryan, is completely unaware of a double entendre, and the other characters, monster and human, poke (pun intended) a bit of fun at him. Since the monster characters are having to tread very lightly to make sure this monster hunter doesn't discover their true identities, the scene takes a moment to show his less intimidating side and that he is, after all, a teenager.

CAPTION: Excerpts from one of *Siren Song's* premium scenes. Developed by STARDUST and protected by United States and international copyright law. © STARDUST.

(*Continued*)

CAPTION (*Continued*): Excerpts from one of *Siren Song's* premium scenes. Developed by STARDUST and protected by United States and international copyright law. © STARDUST.

(*Continued*)

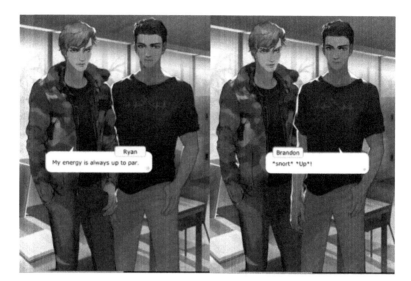

CAPTION (*Continued*): Excerpts from one of *Siren Song's* premium scenes. Developed by STARDUST and protected by United States and international copyright law. © STARDUST.

Dialogue Options. Players can pay to say certain lines of dialogue. These choices lead to longer conversations than nonpremium dialogue choices, they can change relationships with NPCs for better or worse, and/or they can stir up some interesting NPC reactions.

Choice-based game *Insecure: The Come Up Game* has "hype fees" for some of its dialogue choices. These are ways for players to express how they feel about NPCs or show off certain aspects of their personality in conversations. They can be feeling super confident, being sarcastic, etc. Hype fees always elicit responses from NPCs and, sometimes, it can make the NPC like the player more or backfire. Or it's a way for the player to get NPCs to like them less, if that's what they're trying to achieve.

CAPTION: Issa introduces the player to the concept of hype and reacts positively when the player uses hype to talk about herself and negatively when the player doesn't speak well of herself. Screenshots from *Insecure: The Come Up Game*. Developed by Glow Up Games Inc. © 2021 Glow Up Games and Home Box Office Inc.™ All Rights Reserved.

(*Continued*)

CAPTION (*Continued*): Issa introduces the player to the concept of hype and reacts positively when the player uses hype to talk about herself and negatively when the player doesn't speak well of herself. Screenshots from *Insecure: The Come Up Game*. Developed by Glow Up Games Inc. © 2021 Glow Up Games and Home Box Office Inc.™ All Rights Reserved.

(*Continued*)

CAPTION (*Continued*):   Issa introduces the player to the concept of hype and reacts positively when the player uses hype to talk about herself and negatively when the player doesn't speak well of herself. Screenshots from *Insecure: The Come Up Game*. Developed by Glow Up Games Inc. © 2021 Glow Up Games and Home Box Office Inc.™ All Rights Reserved.

(*Continued*)

CAPTION (*Continued*): Issa introduces the player to the concept of hype and reacts positively when the player uses hype to talk about herself and negatively when the player doesn't speak well of herself. Screenshots from *Insecure: The Come Up Game*. Developed by Glow Up Games Inc. © 2021 Glow Up Games and Home Box Office Inc.™ All Rights Reserved.

Skins/Outfits. Players can change what their character wears by paying for new outfits. Premium outfits are immediate ways to get LIs and other NPCs to see the player-character more favorably.

A trope in mobile stories is that NPCs will usually compliment the player on premium outfits and shade them or outright insult their "normal" clothes, if they had the option to change to a premium skin:

Choice A: Buy a new dress.

Choice B: Wear something out of your closet.

Reaction A: Who knew you had such style?

Reaction B: You *have* heard the saying "dress for success," right?

SELECTING ASSETS

Several developers reuse assets across their visual novels that have no relation to each other. This means that a background featuring a lighthouse in a werewolf story can resurface in a slice-of-life romance. Whether you are responsible for writing the outline or you are given an outline from which to work, you might find yourself in the position where you must choose assets for each scene in the visual novel.

If you're writing a new story without ties to a series and you know you'll be working with premade assets, ask to review the background art as you're outlining your story, if the developer doesn't share it with you first. Knowing which backgrounds you have to work with can help you plan the best locations at which your scenes will take place.

In other cases, you'll need to match assets with the developer's outline and scene-by-scene breakdown. While you may only have a handful of backgrounds to choose from, you still want to undergo a thoughtful review of your options. Think about the atmosphere or mood you want to create in the scene and how the background can add to the emotional impact or engagement. How might it add subtext? For example, there are several environments situated at a large park: a jogging trail among the trees, a pond surrounded by benches, and a picnic area. The LI wants to meet with the MC, but he's not ready for his friends to find out they're dating. He wants to see the MC in a secluded place. The best option at the park would be the jogging trail. It's partially hidden by the trees, and it's not as public as the pond or picnic area.

Sometimes, you'll find that where you envision your scene taking place and the available assets aren't the best matches. If you're not able to review assets before you outline your story, try to find locations that may not be perfect, but they're still good fits.

DELIVERING DRAFTS

Like any studio, VN app developers have different ways that they format their scripts. I have followed an outline template housed on Drive for one studio, written a script in Word based on an example script another studio gave me, and had to make up my own way to format the scripts while working with another studio.

If the developer does not have formatting standards for scripts, it will be your responsibility to figure out how you want to format your work. You can determine this with some input from the client on what would be the easiest format for the team to work with. A lot of studios use spreadsheets for their writing because programmers can easily export all the text and import it into the game engine. However, as has been my experience, not every studio works with spreadsheets. The one time I had to determine how best to format my work, I first wrote the chapters in Word, then copied and pasted all of the text and choices into a spreadsheet, and sent both the Word doc and spreadsheet to the producer. I created two versions because the Word doc would be easier for the producer to read and assess the story, and the spreadsheet would be easier for the story's programmer to work with.

Color Coding

Whether you're working in a word processor or a spreadsheet, it helps to color code choices and sections branching off of them. You can also indicate choices that are variable-based, branches of the story that are based on those variables, and branches and variables that lead to different endings. This makes it possible to see how the story is structured at a glance and indicates where branches diverge from the main story, where they end, and where they rejoin the main branch, which also makes it useful for programmers. I implemented this type of formatting when I was a senior editor for choice-based stories that read like e-books, and it was easy for writers who had never worked with branching stories to pick up. What colors you use and how you designate the beginning and ending of a branch is up to you. Just make sure that you're consistent, and your formatting is easy to read.

LOOKING FOR VN WRITING WORK?

If you're looking to write for visual novels, you will need to illustrate that you understand the major structures and characteristics of VNs. The following is advice from developers who've edited and published VNs.

SOUHA AL-SAMKARI, VICE PRESIDENT OF TRUANT PIXEL

Souha Developed VN Akash: Path of the Five.

For visual novels, specifically, I want someone who knows how to convey a lot without going on too long. Visual novels typically have tight restrictions on the amount of text you can display at once, so I want to see writing that is economical but still immerses you. The dialogue should be engaging and not too overblown. If there's branching dialogue in their work, I want to see that they know how to offer fun or meaningful choices to their players. I think that a lot of people aspiring to write for visual novels tend to underestimate the amount of technical skill needed to work in VNs. You need to be able to do a lot with a little, both in terms of text and imagery—you may not always have the artwork you want nor the space to describe something in great length, so you need to be able to paint a picture with fewer words.

WILL HILES, SENIOR NARRATIVE DESIGNER AND WRITER

Will has been an editor for Moments: Choose Your Story *and worked on the initial VN adaptation of Liu Cixin's* The Wandering Earth *for Crazy Maple Studio.*

When looking over a potential visual novel writer's portfolio, I generally have a mental checklist of things I like to see and don't like to see.

First, I take an overview of the types of writing featured. I like to see a variety of genres and styles. Here, I'm trying to get a feel for flexibility and general writing interest. I like well-rounded writers. I like screenwriters. I'm usually turned off by stories that sound the same and that never venture outside of a single genre. However, if I'm looking for a "romance" story, I will pay attention to any of those in that genre and see if it's merely "formula" or if it does something different. Doing something different is always eye-catching.

I first look at samples to see how well a piece is written. I do this whether the writer is a professional, amateur, a narrative designer, self-published or commercially published author. Do I give experienced writers more leeway? Usually, I look at them even closer—they should know better.

I then break this overview down further:

- How is the dialogue—is it natural sounding? Is it appropriate to the story? Is it concise? Does it sound good spoken out loud? Speaking your dialogue out loud is a great test.

- Is the writing showing or telling? Telling is passive. Showing is active and preferred.
- Is there too much exposition? Too much exposition is dull. People tend to skim over it. Exposition is also difficult to translate to a VN.
- Can they tell a story? It doesn't have to have a three-act story structure, but there needs to be a beginning, middle, and an end. Storylines that go nowhere, that resolve nothing, that encounter no obstacles, that require little effort, are to be avoided.
- Can they create relatable, believable characters? Player engagement is dependent on having such characters (hate them, love them, but never be indifferent to them).
- I prefer interactive examples with some branching content, if possible—but it's not mandatory. You can teach branching. If there are branching examples, are the branches meaningful? Are they merely "time wasters?" Do they circle back around to a main storyline, or do they alter the storyline?
- If at all possible, I like to encourage those writers who may not have VN or interactive writing experience but have potential to write something fresh, unexpected, or memorable.

In all, it's a very subjective process, based on my own experience, and what I think makes for a great story.

DELIVERY SCHEDULES

The writing part of production for mobile VNs tends to go quickly. (Depending on the developer, the *entire* production process can go quickly.) For shorter VNs, you may have about 2 weeks to draft the entire story. This schedule is usually based on how long it took past freelancers or employees to complete a story of the same length. I have had anywhere from 2.5 weeks (short VNs) to 3 months (a longer VN) to finish drafts. When you're writing a new, longer story, you may have some flexibility to negotiate your deadlines. However, developers want to add new VNs to their catalogs quickly. Oftentimes, you will not be able to negotiate. You'll just have to go into the project knowing you can deliver the draft in time. Keep in mind that you may still be working on a VN as the first few installments are published.

If you have not written a mobile VN or other choice-based game before, you may be unsure about these deadlines. It does get easier to write drafts the more you do it. Until you have the experience, you might think of comparable writing tasks, like a comics or film script of the same length, or a short story of a similar word count. How long would it take you to finish one of those?

EXERCISES

1. Visual Novel Outlines

     Create an outline template for visual novels.

     How you structure this is up to you. But make sure you have the following elements:

   - arcs,

   - chapters/episodes,

   - scenes per chapter/episode,

   - summaries,

   - choices per scene,

   - premium choices, and

   - premium content.

     If you've written a VN for a mobile studio, it might help you to reverse engineer parts of the story to help you design the template. Just make sure you don't use any of the studio's proprietary information in a finished outline you deliver to another company!

2. Visual Novel Formatting

     Create a structured format for visual novels that you might have to use when developers don't have their own. You may or may not use color coding.

     Consider how to communicate

   - where branches begin and end,

   - where choices have variables,

   - what content is variable-based, and

   - what leads players to certain endings.

NOTES

1 Naturally, use the same language as the developer, whether they refer to installments of the story as chapters, episodes, etc.

2 Michael Dawson, "Designing Episode's Interactive Fiction in Three Phases," Game Developers Conference 2017, uploaded April 27, 2019, YouTube video, 31:17, https://www.youtube.com/watch?v=1Rq2oErDEmA.

CHAPTER 12

Developing Your Own Visual Novels and Choice-Based Games

A Quick Guide

THIS CHAPTER IS FOR individuals or small teams who are planning to make a visual novel or other choice-based project. It includes some things you'll need to keep in mind during your preproduction and some things that you're probably already aware of but that are easy to forget. (I'm speaking from experience here!) Within the chapter, you'll find some additional resources, like an assets checklist and places to find assets that will assist in planning your game. For additional resources, please see "Resources, Planning, and Processes."

When you're the one designing the story, coming up with all the characters and places in the world, and thinking up what sounds you'll need, you are the project's creative lead. So, that's the mindset you need to have going into your preproduction and determining what assets are essential to the game and whom you're going to hire.

DOI: 10.1201/9781003199724-14

We'll look at the types of assets you'll probably need for your game and some ways you can effectively communicate your vision to the team.

SOURCES OF INSPIRATION AND COMMUNICATING YOUR VISION

If you're looking to make your own game, you undoubtedly got the inspiration for it from somewhere or several somewheres. That initial spark of inspiration evolves, and it comes into greater and greater focus as you collaborate with others. While you can simply share your documentation with your team members, it helps if you also communicate your thinking behind the story and the characters. What inspired you in the first place? When they have better insight into what you're doing, they'll have better ideas and conceptualizations as to how to achieve your vision.

Personal Experience

I'm listing personal experience first because, while it's something writers learn in other storytelling media, it's not a source of inspiration or foundation for design that designers and writers often discuss in games. However, we know that what we lived through, people we've known, or places we've been often show up in our storytelling. If anything specific to your lived experience shows up in your game in some form, it can help to share this with your team. It gives them clearer insights into the game, and it also gives them a better understanding of who you are and how you architect your stories.

The more communication between you and your team, the better. That includes them getting clarity about who you are and what's important to you. Let them get excited about the same things that excite you.

Analogues

Another major source of inspiration for our stories and worldbuilding is analogues, whether those analogues are historical figures, major events in history, cultural movements, other stories, etc. Just about anything can serve as an analogue that leads us to use it as a direct inspiration, or it's a point of departure that leads to another idea or concept that ends up in the game.

How you share this information can be formal or informal. If you have actual images or texts that are the basis for places or characters, you'll definitely want to share these in your design and story documentation. If the inspiration is more vague, you might try writing it down to explain it or simply share it in your meetings.

Let your past experiences in game development be your guide. If you've worked on other games before, think about the kind of background information your lead or client shared with you. Then think about the kind of information you *wish* you had known, information that would have made your job much easier at the very start. Provide your team with this content. That doesn't mean that your team members won't want additional background info from you, and it's a good idea to ask them before you begin working with them what kinds of information and references they'll need from you.

ART ASSETS

The most common art assets for visual novels are character sprites, portraits, and backgrounds (the locations the player traverses in the world). You may also have assets like items or objects players can interact with.

Characters

For characters, you will need to communicate with your team how you visualize the main character (MC) and every other character in the game. You can do this through character bios or character sheets and artist references.

Character Bios

A character bio provides information about the character's appearance, their personality, and their history, usually written as encyclopedic content. Parts of a character bio include:

- **Stats:** Traits like race/ethnicity, gender identity, age, height, weight, body type, sexual orientation, eye color, species/race (when the game features non-human characters).

- **Real-Life/Fictional Inspiration:** A real or fictional person the character is based on.

- **Faction/Sect/Organization, Etc.:** Group(s) the character is a part of or swears allegiance to.

- **Attire:** What the character wears and/or a description of their personal style.

- **Personality/Demeanor:** A description of the character's personality and how they carry themselves.

- **Bio/Background/History:** A write-up of the character's life, highlighting what makes them who they are currently.

- **Other Information:** Any information that helps you and your team members get a complete picture of the character. This can include likes/dislikes, hobbies, political beliefs, etc.

You might use some or all of the above in your bios. The background or biographical information can be detailed or more of a character sketch, depending on the needs for the story. For a shorter game, you may not need to go into characters' histories in depth because they won't be relevant to the story or to the characters' development. (You may write up this information for yourself, but your team doesn't need that information. Keep in mind that not everyone is going to want to read a lot of information, especially if it's not relevant to their work.)

You can find a variety of character bio templates online, and you can structure them to fit your needs.[1] You might also consider designing your own character bio template for whenever you have a new project.

Sprite Size
Character sprites can be **full length** (the entire body), **half length** (from the waist up), or other custom sizes, like from the shoulders up.

CAPTION: *999's* half-body sprites (high-definition (HD) remaster). Screenshot from *999*. Developed by Spike Chunsoft and protected by United States and international copyright law. © Spike Chunsoft, Co. Ltd.
RockmanDash12, "Zero Escape: The Nonary Games," Fuwanovel, last accessed April 25, 2022, https://fuwanovel.net/reviews/2017/03/27/zero-escape-the-nonary-games/.

Since portraits are positioned behind text boxes, a few factors will determine the size of your portraits: the positioning of text boxes, how much of the characters' bodies you want within view, and your budget. The larger the drawing, the more it will cost. So, full-body portraits are going to be the most expensive. However, while budget is something you have to keep in mind, you'll also consider onscreen presentation.

CAPTION: Half-body sprite by Star Anise VN.

CAPTION: Full-body sprites by Mr. Curcurbita.

Some questions to keep in mind to help you determine what size portraits you'll want:

- How much of the screen's real estate do text boxes cover? Would players be able to see a character's legs? Or would the text box cover them up?

- Will you be using character sprites in scenes without text boxes?

- What do you personally prefer? Do you prefer the look of full-body or half-body characters, or another size?

Camera Angles and Character Positions

Character sprites have different onscreen positions. Think of players sitting in front of their screens or looking at their phones while engaging with your game. Characters can be facing players head on or looking at them from different side angles, or they might look at the player from more of a three-quarter view. Their bodies can be positioned to face the player directly or not. Your artist(s) will need to know at what angles to draw characters. (If you're not sure what angles or positions you need or if you should use certain angles/positions for specific scenes, these are great question to ask the artist.)

Camera Angles:

- Front

- Side

- Back

- Three quarter

- Rear three quarter

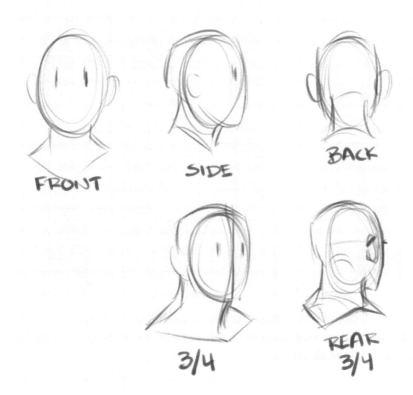

CAPTION: Camera angle sketches by JB Fuller. © Untethered Studios.

Along with head and body positions, also think about in which direction the character is looking. If the MC is offscreen (and a stand-in for the player), then characters might be looking in the player's direction. They could be looking at other onscreen characters, or they could be looking away from characters. Where they look can say a lot about how they feel about other characters in the scene or where they are emotionally. Are they being evasive by looking away, are they shy, are they just in a bad mood and don't want to be bothered, etc.? In a moment of confrontation, it would make sense for the non-player character (NPC) to face the MC (and the player by extension) head on. The motivation for where characters are looking is also part of their emotional states, which you may include in their character designs.

CAPTION: *Incarnō: Everything Is Written* sprites for Nick, who always feels down on his luck and stressed, and can't figure out why. Art by JB Fuller, Untethered Studios. © Schnoodle Studio.

Emotional States

What emotions are characters feeling with each line of dialogue they speak? How are they reacting to certain situations and/or things other characters are saying? Consider how characters' expressions are going to change throughout a scene. Dialogue and scene scenarios can suggest what characters are feeling at any given moment, but visuals accompanying these scenarios make characters feel like more realized individuals.

You might want to map out these different emotional states in the script. As I'm writing a script, I'll note in parentheses the character's emotion while speaking the line. When I have my final draft, I'll go back through the script and make a list of emotions I've noted for each character and also look for places where I can add emotional states for unspoken reactions.

> VINCENT (smirking/smiling): Yeah, I guess you've earned it.
>
> NARRATOR: I stretch and yawn. Didn't sleep last night, either.
>
> VINCENT: Imma head out too.

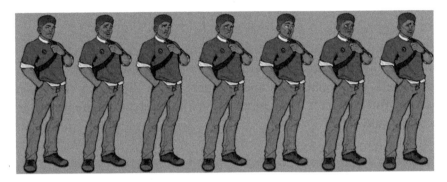

CAPTION: My noting Vincent's emotional states in the script and Vincent's sprites with different emotional states. Art by JB Fuller, Untethered Studios. © Schnoodle Studio.

You don't have to use my method. What makes the most sense for you and is the easiest way for you to catalog all of the emotional states you might need?

Like other aspects of the characters' designs, what your story requires, what you wish to communicate to players, and your budget will factor in to how many emotional states you'll need per character. The characters' importance to the story and their screen time may determine the various number of character sprites with different emotional states you create for them. So, the MC may have the most sprites by far, another main character might have quite a few, and a secondary character may have one or two. Each character can have bespoke emotions, based upon their involvement in the story. Or you might have a more generic set of emotional states like neutral, happy, sad, angry, and surprised, and every character gets sprites for these emotions.

Physical States

Does anything change about your characters' physical appearances throughout the game? While eating, do they get food on their shirts? Do they get wet, and this is noted by other characters or makes up an important scene? If you have important character moments or changes in a character's physical appearance are important to the plot, you might want to reflect this in the character's sprite or portrait.

Same as a review of the script for all of your characters' emotional states, you can also look for moments when their physical appearances change. Then decide whether those changes are important enough to reflect in their art.

Offscreen Portraits

Character portraits also feature prominently in or near the text box. These are typically headshots or other partial images. These portraits illustrate characters' emotional states and reactions when they don't appear onscreen. You may have this type of portrait for each of a character's emotional states.

CAPTION: Ash's offscreen portrait (*The Letter*). Developed by Yangyang Mobile and protected by United States and international copyright law. © Yangyang Mobile.

"The Letter: A Horror Visual Novel," EastAsiaSoft, accessed April 28, 2022, https://www.eastasiasoft.com/games/The-Letter-A-Horror-Visual-Novel.

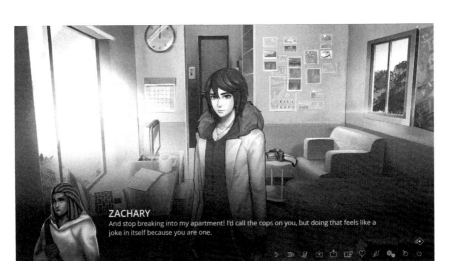

CAPTION: Zach's offscreen portrait (*The Letter*). Developed by Yangyang Mobile and protected by United States and international copyright law. © Yangyang Mobile.
"The Letter," Visual Novel Database, accessed April 28, 2022, https://vndb.org/v18550.

Locations and Background Art

Most VNs are two-dimensional with static backgrounds. They're representations of locations within the game's world. Players will see a VN's backgrounds multiple times throughout the story. If you think about it, this is the same as the experience with non-VNs. Even in open world games, players will visit the same locations many times.

Every place players can visit, explore, or interact with needs background art. (Of course, 3D environments are also possible, although the focus here is on 2D environments.)

A Sense of Place

Background art is an immediate way to establish the world visually and reveal where the player will be traveling in the world. Narrative text can explain what the world is like to the player but not as quickly as an onscreen image that stays in front of the player until they move to the next location. Backgrounds quickly set the physical and psychological atmosphere.

If you see a bright, sunny day outside of a school, you'll have a very different idea about the world than if the scene were set inside of a dimly lit bar in a subbasement. As a player, you don't need text to tell you a game partly takes place in a school and will feature student characters, but the *image* of the school on a bright, sunny day gives players a feeling about what kind of environment this place is and whether characters attending and instructing there are friendly or not. You can reinforce player expectations based upon that image or subvert them.

I made a short VN with point-and-click mechanics, *Vanished*, for Global Game Jam in 2019. The settings I chose as backgrounds are royalty-free photos with Creative Commons licenses, and I used a filter on them. I wanted to get across the mystery, magic, and a sense of an abandoned or lost civilization. However, this appearance works against the player's expectations. The world is not abandoned, even though its architecture is crumbling, and there are no people, animals, or vegetation. In searching the environment, the player will break a spell and reveal a couple of inhabitants who've been hiding and hibernating in the town.

CAPTION: A seemingly abandoned courtyard. Screenshot from *Vanished*. © Toiya Kristen Finley.

CAPTION: When breaking a spell in a certain order, the player first finds a soldier. Screenshot from *Vanished*. © Toiya Kristen Finley.

CAPTION: After the soldier awakens, a young woman confronts the player. Screenshot from *Vanished*. © Toiya Kristen Finley.

Background art reinforces the story you're telling through narration and dialogue, even if it's a still image that never changes.

Another benefit of visual novel backgrounds is that players may not see everything in the background art the first few times they go to the location. So, imagine their surprise when they see something new and get more insight about that place or simply realize there was more to the art than they initially thought.

This background from *Incarnō: Everything Is Written* is the audience at a press conference. It's a predominantly Black audience (the audience's makeup is never mentioned), and there are Black hairstyles represented in the silhouettes. A player may not recognize this at first.

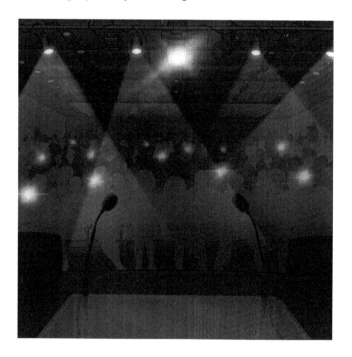

CAPTION: Art by Eleanor Grootch. © Schnoodle Studio.

Associating Characters and Scenarios with Locations

A language of expectation develops between the VN and the player when characters and other parts of the story become associated with a particular location. *Hatoful Boyfriend* has several locations that are specific to certain characters. If players are looking to find those characters or engage with them, they go to those locations. Additionally, the MC engages in specific behaviors or activities at certain locations. Players knowing that they can go to a particular location to interact with a character or perform an action is something writers can use to their advantage. For example, we can design character routes or nested branches where players looking to complete or "find" a character route have to visit locations associated with that character.

Designing Locations

When designing the looks of these locations, keep both their **functions/ purposes** and **associations** in mind. The functions or purposes point to how individuals use the location. If I'm designing a library, I'm imagining a space where its purpose is to house collections of books, periodicals, and microfiche. Its purpose is to provide visitors the ability to research numerous subjects, study, attend meetings for classes or projects, or give them a quiet place to read. But at this particular library, there's also a secret society of librarian necromancers who protect ancient tomes detailing how to defeat the dead (the library's **association**). At first glance, the library looks like one you might find on a campus or in a neighborhood. But if you look closely, you might see a water bottle with the secret society's logo on it.

Depending on your project's gameplay and mechanics, locations may have extra functions. For example, most of the locations players visit in *Monster Prom* are classes. Each time players go to that class, they'll increase one of their stats.

CAPTION: Gym class nets players +2 Charm per visit. Screenshot from *Monster Prom*. Developed by Beautiful Glitch and protected by United States and international copyright law. © Beautiful Glitch.

Some Questions for Designing Locations

Should the Background Change to Reflect What's Happening in a Scene? Based on my library, the librarian necromancers convene for meetings at different points in the story. They might put an incantation on the wall to keep visitors away before each meeting, and on the checkout counter, they place a punch bowl and tray of cookies for meeting refreshments.

What Clues Can You Give Players about What Goes on at the Location? These may not always be visual, especially if certain characters are associated with the location, like certain characters going to the library turning out to be librarian necromancers. However, you can leave little clues about who inhabits or frequents the location or how it's used. For example, there's a water bottle on the table with the secret society's logo on it.

What Clues Can You Give Players about Characters Who Inhabit or Frequent That Location? Does the location reveal anything about their identities or motives? Players discover the librarians' secret society. Later, they run into a character there whom they've never seen at the library before. This would help players connect the dots or begin to wonder if the character is a member of that secret society. Clues don't have to be large reveals or huge, worldbuilding details. Think about characters' living spaces. What kind of furniture is in them? Are these spaces neat or messy? Do they have art on the walls, and what kind? Do they have knick-knacks on wall shelves, etc.? Use your characters' personalities, hobbies, likes, dislikes, and obsessions to create the places where they live.

Are Locations Connected to Mechanics? As is the case with *Monster Prom*, do locations increase stats? If you're working on an adventure game or hidden-object game, like *Vanished*, the player will need to interact with the art. Make a list of all the objects/items in a location (or scene) that are parts of puzzles or that players will need to interact with in order to learn valuable information. Now, add some more objects/items serving as red herrings (in other words, they help to populate the location, add opportunities to include lore or flavor text,[2] and also give the player some "wrong answers" to puzzles).

At What Time(s) of Day Does the Story Take Place at the Location?
Players can go to locations multiple times during a playthrough, and they can visit these places at different times during the day. If the location only appears in the story during the afternoon, then you'll only need an afternoon version of the location. However, if the player can go to the location during the afternoon and night, you will need afternoon and night versions. The lighting and shading for the versions will be different. You might also think about other ways the location changes during the day. Back to the library hiding the librarian necromancers, during the day, they don't bring out their stacks of books they use for spell casting. After hours, those books are up front on the floor and stacked high on tables.

If you're not an artist who's never had to really think of detailing what an environment looks like, designing a location can seem intimidating at first. If you have a mental picture, start there. Jot down what's at the location. What colors do you see or would you like to use? Think about who uses the space and why. Look up similar references to see who and what populates similar places. Use these to flesh out your location with details you may not have considered.

A NOTE ON ARTIST REFERENCES

Just about anything can serve as references for your artist(s), sound designer(s), and composer(s), and you should collect these references for all of your art, whether those references are for characters, locations, computer graphics (CGs), user interface (UI), or logos. Also, keep in mind that every reference doesn't have to be visual. If you're trying to get across a certain feeling or atmosphere, you might use songs or sound effects.

What has often been frustrating for me is that I sometimes can't find the references that express what I'm going for, despite lots of research and hunting for them. I've learned not to pick references that are "good enough." In other words, I couldn't find exactly what I wanted, but I did find something that was *sorta, kinda?* what I was picturing. Giving artists "good enough" references is a mistake, even if you tell them, "This is not quite what I want" because you've now given them something concrete that they will be using, and this less-satisfactory thing is now in their minds as a reference. If you're struggling to find the right references, tell your artist and then explain as best you can to them what you're visualizing.

Be sure to ask what kind of references everyone needs and prefers. I've worked with a sound designer who needs visual references, not just an idea of what something should sound like.

CGs

The important pieces of art players unlock at certain points in the story, CGs are rewards for befriending or romancing certain characters, finishing a certain route or getting an ending, or reaching a significant moment. If you include CGs, you want them to feel special when players unlock them.

An important note about CGs: For a lot of games, the CGs are of a different style or aesthetic than the in-scene characters and environments. This points to them being special, unlocked content, or captured moments. These differing styles also give you the opportunity to present characters from another perspective (literally). They can be in a more romantic or intimate light or more menacing or terrifying, depending on the mood, scene, or ending.

CAPTION: Alkar's in-scene and CG art from *When the Night Comes*. Developed by Lunaris Games and protected by United States and international copyright law. © Lunaris Games.

(Continued)

CAPTION (*Continued*):   Alkar's in-scene and CG art from *When the Night Comes.*
Developed by Lunaris Games and protected by United States and international
copyright law. © Lunaris Games.

Note how in the CG, Alkar is directly facing players and is positioned
much closer to them than in the scene.

Here are some ideas to help you determine what you should depict in
CGs:

- **How Do You Give Each of Your Endings Closure?** You might illustrate the scenario for each ending, or you can show the player what
  happens *after* the story ends. (Include any hidden/secret endings!)

- **What Are Character-Defining Moments?** CGs can enhance something that has changed in someone's characterization.

- **What Moments Does the MC Share with an NPC?** Players work hard to improve (or wreck!) relationships for certain NPCs, so the CG showing a change in a relationship is a great reward. If the CG depicts an LI who is in a good relationship with the MC, it could be intimate. The CG can illustrate the MC and NPC together, or just the NPC.

- **What Pivotal Moments Do NPCs Share?** CGs can also depict important moments between NPCs. Do their relationships change? Do they have intense or lighthearted moments? Do they have a shared experience?

- **Can the CG Stand in for a Cutscene?** You may not have animation, but a CG can be a still image that represents a transition in the plot or action.

CAPTION: One of *Monster Prom's* endings, players get a CG of Miranda turning them down after they ask her out to prom. Developed by Beautiful Glitch and protected by United States and international copyright law. © Beautiful Glitch.

MUSIC/SOUNDTRACK

Listening to accompanying music is an important part of the player's experience. Unfortunately, sometimes studios (including the really, really large ones) leave reaching out to composers to score the game to the very last minute. Your game's music deserves as much thought and care as art and UI. It not only creates atmospheric soundscapes, but it also engages players in ways that art and text cannot.

Your game's overall themes, characters, places in the world, and plot points can all serve as inspirations for the soundtrack. Think about what tracks will play during certain scenes, at certain locations, when certain characters are onscreen, or during certain moments. Music is part of your storytelling too, so focus on how a track can highlight, communicate, or set a vibe.

Do characters and locations get their own theme songs? Do you have tracks for certain emotions or themes? For example, if something suspicious is afoot or a character is puzzling over something, there might be a theme for that. There may be a lighthearted or whimsical theme for sillier, less serious moments.

It's important to share everything you can about the story with the composer. This includes characters and their story arcs, what's happening in pivotal scenes, and the places where players will travel. Musical inspirations and influences are also key references to share. Do you have a soundtrack you're listening to for inspiration as you write? Talk about that and why it's helping you with the story.

If a composer isn't in your budget, there are media websites that offer royalty-free music or music with a Creative Commons license. Some of these websites are

- Pixabay <pixabay.com>,

- Free Music Archive <freemusicarchive.org>,

- Free Stock Music <free-stock-music.com>, and

- Mixkit <mixkit.co>.

 Welcome to all **free music** seekers and thanks for stopping by! Here, you can find **royalty-free music** for your YouTube videos or projects (blog, vlog, podcast, social network, etc.). All we ask is to put the attribution in the credits. More info about the attribution can be found on every track's page. The free music on this website is not a subject to any copyright issues. If you need royalty free background music for your business or everyday life, work and play activities, feel free to use our curated collection of Royalty Free Music Playlists.

CAPTION: Free Stock Music's attribution requirements.

Depending on the composer, they may or may not require that you give them attribution. So, make sure you do include the correct attribution and the wording the artist requires. There are also royalty-free websites that require you to pay for a license if you want to use their music in commercial projects. While you'll have to pay, this can still be an affordable option.

SOUND EFFECTS

Sound effects are similar to music, in that you can overlook thinking about their involvement. Sound effects often accompany player interaction with UI elements, like clicking. Major moments or notable changes tend to have sound effects, too. For example, a hidden door creaks open.

Other Types of Sound Effects

- **Ambient Sound:** The background sounds in a scene or at a location. A slight breeze at a park, conversational chatter at a mall, spoons clanking against coffee cups at a café, etc.

- **Dialogue Text Effects:** Effects to simulate the sound of characters talking. There may be one text effect for all characters. Or each character may get their own effect, with pitch, speed, and tonal differences. Some text effects are so memorable that players can tell who's "talking" just by hearing their text effect.

- **Emotes/Onomatopes:** Characters' non-verbal utterances, like "hmm," "ahhh," "uhhh …," or short phrases that establish the emotional tone of a line. Sometimes, characters will have their own voiced catchphrases, like Hugo of *Dream Daddy's* "Sweet manchego!"

- **Scene Transitions:** A sound to signal players are moving from one scene to the next, like a swoosh or chime.

It's sort of a refrain by now, but your budget will come into play if you're looking to pay a sound designer. How many sound effects can you afford? Which sound effects are absolutely essential for the experience you're designing?

Like royalty-free music, royalty-free sound effects are also available. You can find some of them at

- Pixabay,

- Mixkit,

- Freesound <freesound.org>, and

- Zapsplat <zapsplat.com>.

DESIGNING SCENES

A lot of work goes into composing a scene. Not only are you keeping track of which characters should appear in the scene, but you'll also need to note sound effects and specific music tracks to use. You'll need this information for yourself, and you'll also need to share it with your team so that they implement the correct assets. Planning out your scenes has the added benefit of informing you about all of the assets the game requires.

Some Considerations for Designing Scenes:

Think about Onscreen Presentation. This is about the overall aesthetics of the screen: where you position text boxes, how players interact with the onscreen elements, etc.

What Is the Maximum Number of Characters You'll Have on Screen at One Time? Usually, this is four. Think about the total number of characters that can fit comfortably before the screen looks crowded.

What Time of Day Is It? Is it the morning, afternoon, or night? Make sure that the location used in the scene matches the time of day.

How Will Characters Be Positioned on Screen? At what camera angles are character sprites positioned? This affects where their gaze is directed and how their bodies are positioned.

Will Characters Be Full Body or Half Body or Another Size? How much of the character sprite does the player need to see? How much of the screen does the text box cover, and how does this affect the character sprite's size?

What Are Characters' Emotional States? Are the characters' emotions changing? Are they responding to what other characters are saying or to the present situation in which they find themselves?

What Background Music Will You Use? What tracks match the mood of the scene? Do you have theme songs for particular characters or locations?

Does the Music's Volume Change During the Scene? You can raise the volume to meet the right emotional tone. Maybe something suspenseful is happening, there's a major revelation you're highlighting, or you want to sweep the player up in an emotional moment for a character or characters.

Are You Using Any Sound Effects? What sound effects make sense for the scene? How loud should the sound effects be?

UI ASSETS

If the game doesn't have puzzle or exploration mechanics, the UI is the major way players interact with the game. They click or tap portions of text boxes to advance to the next bit of text. They click on NPC and MC dialogue text boxes to get to the next line of dialogue, piece of narration, or choice. They click on or tap choices to make decisions. They tap the "skip" button to fast-forward through scenes and choices they've made before to get to choice points where they haven't made one of the choices. But there are other menus that are important features of visual novels. The CG gallery is where players can view all of the CGs they've unlocked during their playthroughs. If players can unlock music tracks, you can give them a menu where they can listen to the music. Or you might include in one of your menus the endings the player has unlocked, and each ending may need its own art.

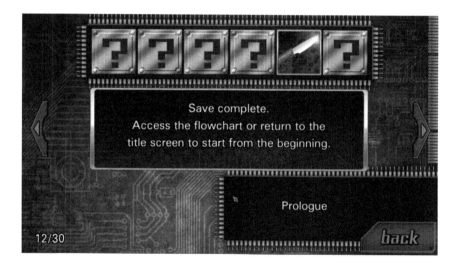

CAPTION: *999's* unlocked endings and corresponding art are included in the save menu. Screenshot from *999*. Developed by Spike Chunsoft and protected by United States and international copyright law. © Spike Chunsoft, Co. Ltd. Materwelonz, "Let's Play 999: 9 Hours, 9 Persons, 9 Doors [PC Remaster] Blind Part 15: Zero Escape: Nonary Games," uploaded April 17, 2017, YouTube video, 1:02:15, https://www.youtube.com/watch?v=OuUM6CjeXPw.

There are several types of text boxes you might incorporate:

- **Narration:** All of the "novel-like" text, including the MC's thoughts and observations in prose form, NPC descriptions, scene setting, and exposition. Another type of narration text box is one that players can open to read the last few lines of the story, including lines based on their choices. This is useful if the player wants to make a mental recap of what's just happened, has missed something and wants to understand what's happening, or needs to make a choice and needs some context for the decision.

- **Dialogue:** Text boxes for lines of dialogue. These can be character-specific, with the name of the speaker appearing somewhere on or in the text box. If the name of the character is unknown, the name usually appears as "???." These text boxes may also include a character portrait of the speaking character, with or without an emotional state.

- **Choices:** Both dialogue and actions. Choice text boxes can be the same for dialogue choices and action choices, or choices text boxes can be specific to the type of choice. If players can make choices based on the MC having a high enough stat or a certain ability, think about greying out/locking and unlocking those choices. The number of choices players might make at any time may also change. There may only be one choice on the screen (a continue button, basically) or many, based upon how you've designed your branching and choice system.

Other standard menus include:

- **Main Screen:** Where players start a new game, continue a current playthrough, or access other game menus.

- **Save Settings:** Where players can access all of their playthrough saves.

- **Credits:** The listing of everyone who worked on the game and their titles/roles.

The UI needs a unifying aesthetic that ties together all UI elements, menus, and fonts. That doesn't mean the UI design can't be simple and clean, but it does have to be consistent. Remember, as well, that every part of the game has the potential to be a vehicle of story delivery, so the UI can be a part of the game's narrative design. An excellent non-VN example of this is the *Mass Effect* franchise. The UI in all of the games looks like the user interface for a spaceship. Why? The player-character in every game is responsible for a spaceship and its crew. The UI reflects the player-character's characterization and role and the world of the game.

I mentioned in "The Story Delivery of Visual Novels" that I wanted *Incarnō's* UI to be representative of the ancient, mysterious book of the same name. So, there are details in all of the menus and screen elements that are inspired by the book's aesthetic.

CAPTION: The mood board *Incarnō's* UI designer Jules Riseling developed based upon my references and her additional research, and the resulting main menu screen. © Schnoodle Studio.

GAME LOGO

The game logo is a marketing tool for the game. It appears both inside and outside of the game. Expect to use your game logo on store pages, social media, in press releases, in slide decks, as a watermark, and on merch.

Anyone who sees the logo should get a sense about the game's themes, story, and/or aesthetic. It does not have to reference any one character or plot point, although it could. *Undertale's* logo features a pixilated font and a red heart. The font evokes the game's art style, and the heart, an important motif appearing again and again in the game, represents the player-character's soul.

CAPTION: With *Incarnō's* logo, I wanted to reference the symbol on *Incarnō* the book without using that exact same symbol. Logo design by Eduardo Zaldivar. © Schnoodle Studio.

The game logo is your opportunity to decide what you want to emphasize about your game at a glance. There's no right or wrong here. If you're not sure, discuss this with your logo designer. For more information, "Designing Game Logos" is a great resource for insight behind a team's process.[3]

ASSETS CHECKLIST

This is a checklist for common assets found in visual novels and other interactive fiction games. Every project is unique, so you may require additional types of assets.

CHARACTERS
- MC (angles, emotional states, half or full body)
- NPCs (angles, emotional states, half or full body)

LOCATIONS

- All places players will visit
- Variations for times of day (morning, afternoon, night)

CGs

- Unlockable illustrations/art that appear in game

UI

- Text boxes
  - dialogue (MC and NPC)
  - choices (action and dialogue)
  - narration
  - "previous" text (the player can go back and look at the last few lines of the story, including dialogue or narration based on their choices)
- Choice buttons
- Skip button
- "Next" or scroll button (advance to next text box)
- Main menu
- Settings
- CG gallery
- Unlocked music tracks
- Menus for other collectibles

MUSIC/SOUNDTRACK

- All tracks in the game
- Character and location themes
- Tracks for pivotal moments

SOUND EFFECTS

- UI interactions
- Ambient sounds
- Dialogue text sound effects
- Emotes/onomatopes
- Screen transitions

GAME LOGO

- Marketing representation outside and inside the game

HIRING TEAM MEMBERS

Knowing what assets you need is great, but where do you find programmers, artists, and designers? There are a lot of talented people out there, but not everyone is right for your team. Where do you start?

BEYOND TALENT AND SKILLS …

Developers might have fantastic portfolios and skills, but that doesn't mean they're going to be the right fit. There are other considerations when it comes to bringing someone on to your project and paying them. Souha Al-Samkari is the Vice President of Truant Pixel and developer of *Akash: Path of the Five*. Here are her thoughts:

Aside from the quality of the work, first and foremost, you need to see if your would-be contractors have (A) experience, (B) follow-through, and (C) communication skills. Experience can sometimes be a good indicator of points B and C, but not always. Sometimes, experience doesn't translate from job to job, or sometimes, the circumstances are simply different in some crucial way. What you need to know is whether or not this person can deliver work, consistently, on time, and communicate effectively throughout. Someone who is slower to deliver but keeps you updated is going to be better than someone who can deliver five pieces up front and then disappears halfway into production because they've gotten overwhelmed and can't manage to tell you so.

Things to look out for: people who don't have a clear estimation of their own ability to produce, people with a lack of/loose professional and personal boundaries, people who spend a lot of their time publicly getting in fights online on their professional accounts, and people who denigrate the work of their industry peers.

Finding Talent

Referrals are gold. If you have friends or acquaintances who've developed their own games, ask who they'd recommend. You can then reach out to their referrals, or they may introduce you. I've worked with several developers because of referrals.

If you've attended game jams and had good experiences collaborating with people, reach out to them and find out if they'd like to work on your project.

Whose work have you liked on other games? Look for their online portfolios or other ways to contact them online.

There are also websites like Reddit where developers post their work and Discord servers that are dedicated to game development and game genres. Not only can you see developers' work, but you can also get a sense of how they approach their creative process and their personalities.

HOW SHOULD I FORMAT MY WORK?

As we covered, there are a number of ways to format your scripts: Excel or Google spreadsheets, Word or Google docs, Final Draft, Twine files, ink files, etc. Since this is your project, you're in charge of how all of the documents will be formatted.

This is something you'll also want to discuss with your programmer(s). What's most convenient for *them*? What format can they work with the best in order to get all of the different kinds of text (narration, dialogue, choices, lore, etc.) into the game?

You might have one format available for the programmers (like a spreadsheet) and a more traditional script in Final Draft or a Word doc for the rest of the team members to use as a reference.

LIMITED ASSETS AREN'T A LIMITATION

Most visual novels are simple in their presentation. This is *not* a weakness. Other games may have thousands of assets (and the money behind them to create all of those assets), but VN players expect fewer assets. The limited number of assets VN writers and designers may have to work with on any given project can be a *strength*. You can use how the visuals and game mechanics of VNs communicate with players to your advantage and find unique ways of telling your story, while creating a new language of expectation between your game and players.

While the role of creative lead may be a new challenge for you, it gives you a lot of command in determining what gets into your game. There are a lot of moving parts in a game development, and it might be difficult or a little overwhelming to keep track of them all. If you have experience working on games (whether that was a student project, game jams, or with a studio as an employee or freelancer), think about all of the different departments or team members who had a hand in making assets and storytelling. That will give you a good idea when planning your own storytelling and narrative design.

If you *don't* have this experience, it's not a hindrance! Play a game that's similar to yours—it may be the same game genre or story genre. Analyze the scene building, what makes up a scene, how characters are designed, what you hear, how you interact with the screen, etc. Now, reverse engineer your analysis to see which of these elements you can also implement into your own project.

EXERCISE

Start putting together a list of all the assets you will need in your game. You may not be able to complete this in one sitting, as you'll realize you forgot some things, or aspects of the game change, and you'll need to revise your list by adding or subtracting assets.

Review "Assets Checklist" earlier in the chapter as a guide.
Types of Assets You Will Need:

- Characters
- Background art
- CGs
- UI
- Sound effects
- Music
- Game logo(s)

NOTES

1 *The Game Narrative Toolbox's* companion website has a character bio template under its templates section, which you can download as a ZIP file: https://routledgetextbooks.com/textbooks/9781138787087/default.php. You can tailor it to fit your characters and projects.
2 Lore is text about the world that can be found just about anywhere in the game and can cover anything regarding the world, its history, the people within it, or its culture. You can write lore in any style or tone to fit the game's aesthetic. Lore can be written as poetry, jokes, journal entries, advertisements, pamphlets—whatever you need to communicate a certain aspect of the world (a location, character, creature, weapon, etc.).
3 Simon Dean, "Designing Game Logos," Game Developer, April 25, 2013, https://www.gamedeveloper.com/art/designing-game-logos.

CHAPTER 13

Resources, Planning, and Processes

THERE ARE MANY DIFFERENT angles in which to tackle outlining, formatting, writing, and communicating to a team the visual novel's (VN) writing and design. Because of this, I don't want to give you just my perspective or the way I do things. The way I do things may not quite make sense for how your brain works or your communication style. So, here, Michelle Clough and I will share some of our techniques and provide some resources for writing VNs and other choice-based games. Michelle is the chair of the International Game Developers Association's Romance and Sexuality Special Interest Group and has experience working on VNs for both PC and mobile. She was an editor, playtester, and additional writer for *1931: Scheherazade at the Library of Pergamum*; she was the editor of *Purrfect Date,* and the writer of *Open Heart 3* for Choices. She also wrote two text-based, interactive fictions for Sana Stories, *The Tower of Shalott* and *Bonds of the Ninja* (full disclosure: I edited both).

The resources listed here are not exhaustive, so you may find other tools that you or your team find easier to work with, or they're better for the game you're designing.

DOI: 10.1201/9781003199724-15

VISUAL NOVEL ENGINES

You can write and program VNs within engines like Unity and Unreal, but there are engines built specifically for making VNs. These take into account the characteristics of VNs, like their story delivery, branching structure, choice design, and variables, and you can implement all of your game's assets. All of these engines have free tutorials which you can follow on YouTube.

Ren'Py

Ren'Py, written in Python, is an open-source and free-for-commercial-use engine specifically for programming VNs and life sims. Its scripting language is for nonprogrammers so that they can quickly pick it up. *Doki Doki Literature Club!* was made in Ren'Py.

```
label family:
    scene bg beach2
    with dissolve

    "It wasn't long before Mary broke the silence, by asking me a question."

    show mary dark smiling
    with dissolve

    m "I told you a little about my family... but I haven't asked you about yours yet. What's your family like?"

    p "When I'm on the island here, I live with my aunt and uncle, but back home, I live with my mother, father, and sister."

    m "A sister? Is she older or younger?"
```

CAPTION: Ren'Py's scripting language, as demonstrated on the website. "Why Ren'Py?" Renpy.org, accessed May 11, 2022, https://www.renpy.org/why.html.

Website: https://www.renpy.org/
Additional Reading:
Game Development with Ren'Py: Introduction to Visual Novel Games Using Ren'Py, TyranoBuilder, and Twine, Robert Cisela (Apress, 2019).

TyranoBuilder

TyranoBuilder is a visual editor (or visual coder),[1] meaning there is no programming necessary. The engine was developed for nonprogrammers and uses a drag-and-drop interface.

CAPTION: TyranoBuilder's interface.
"Home," Tyranobuilder.com, accessed May 11, 2022, https://tyranobuilder.com/.

Website: https://tyranobuilder.com/
Additional Reading:
Game Development with Ren'Py: Introduction to Visual Novel Games Using Ren'Py, TyranoBuilder, and Twine, Robert Cisela (Apress, 2019).

Fungus (Unity Add-On)

Fungus is a free and open-source Unity add-on, meaning you use it within the Unity engine. While it's not specifically for visual novels, it is a visual coding tool made for choice-based and branching games. *Dream Daddy: A Dad Dating Simulator* and *Purrfect Date: Cat Island* were scripted in Fungus.[2]

CAPTION: Clock Work Raven Studios demonstrates developing their demo in Fungus. © Clock Work Raven Studios.

Ashley Rezvani, "Putting the Fun in Fungus," ClockWorkRavenStudios.com, August 5, 2021, https://www.clockworkravenstudios.com/blog/putting-the-fun-in-fungus.

Website: https://fungusgames.com/

SCRIPTING LANGUAGES AND STORY ENGINES

These are more general programs you can use for writing visual novels, and you can then implement your scripts into engines like Unity, Unreal, GDevelop, etc. All of these engines have free tutorials, which you can find on YouTube.

Twine

Twine is effective for designing complicated branching or prototypes. It's easy to use and has an intuitive interface reminiscent of notes connected by string. If you have scripting knowledge, you can integrate art, sound, and movie assets in Twine.

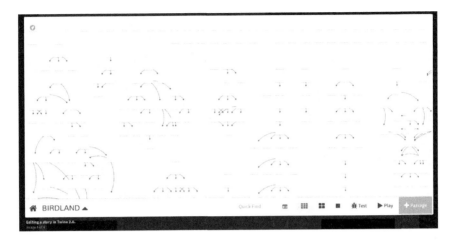

🏠 BIRDLAND ▲   Quick Find   📷   ⊞   ▦   ■   🎲 Test   ▶ Play   ➕ Passage

Editing a story in Twine 2.0.
Image 6 of 4

CAPTION: A screenshot of Twine 2.0 from Twine's website.
Twine homepage, accessed May 12, 2002, https://twinery.org/.

Website: https://twinery.org/
Additional Reading:

- *Writing Interactive Fiction with Twine: Playing Inside a Story*, Melissa Ford (Que Publishing, 2016)

- *Game Development with Ren'Py: Introduction to Visual Novel Games Using Ren'Py, TyranoBuilder, and Twine*, Robert Cisela (Apress, 2019)

ink

ink is a narrative scripting language, which uses a text-based narrative engine designed for writers to use with ease. ink can also be integrated into Unity projects. Studios use ink for their choice-based games. Visual novel *NeoCab* was made with ink.

CAPTION: Scripting for *80 Days* in ink.
"ink: A Narrative Scripting Language for Games," InkleStudios.com, accessed
May 11, 2020, https://www.inklestudios.com/ink/.

Website: https://www.inklestudios.com/ink/
Additional Reading:

- *ink: The Official User's Guide*, Jon Ingold and Joseph Humfrey (inkle studios, 2022)

- *Dynamic Story Scripting with the ink Scripting Language*, Daniel Cox (Packt Publishing, 2021)

Yarn Spinner

It is also designed with writers in mind, and it is specifically used for
dialogue and branching narrative. Users will have to know some coding.

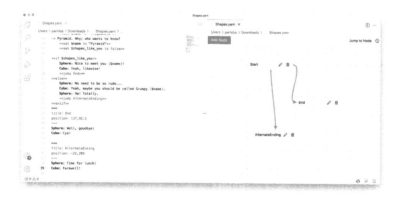

CAPTION: Screenshot from Yarn Spinner's website.
"Editing with VS Code," Yarnspinner.dev, accessed May 12, 2022, https://docs.
yarnspinner.dev/getting-started/editing-with-vs-code.

Website: https://yarnspinner.dev/

PLANNING

Brainstorming and Outlining

There are multiple techniques for brainstorming. Free association (writing down whatever comes to mind in relation to a word or concept without self-editing) and mind mapping (taking a concept or idea and drawing lines from that idea to connected ideas) are some common ones. If you're working with a client or team or you're given the barebones story, brainstorming concepts and story ideas will probably be easier than coming up with the story entirely by yourself. You can use some of the themes, story beats, plot points, or references to build upon.

Don't overlook the role of research and the inspiration it brings. Oftentimes, simply by looking up one thing, I'll get ideas for several others, or an initial thought I have gets shaped and refined by what I discover.

Visualizing is also a big part of my brainstorming process (and writing process, too, to be honest). I view my stories like films in my head, and I can start visualizing anytime anywhere. I can hear the characters, so I go over their dialogue and the action until I'm happy with the scene. When I'm doing this *intentionally*, I prefer at night in the dark (so I can see the pictures more clearly) and listen to music, which sort of serves as a soundtrack. During the brainstorming process when I'm still trying to figure out what the story is, I may not see scenes or characters clearly. So, when I get a blip of an image, I play around with it to develop the scene and "write" it as I'm visualizing it. Sometimes, it takes me a while to understand a character, and visualizing them in these scenes allows me to get some notes on their personalities and voice. Later, when I'm writing through visualizing, I'll go over scenes I know will be in the story over and over and over until they make sense, and I really understand who the characters are. Sometimes, I even unintentionally memorize the dialogue until I write it down!

Whether you're big into outlining or you "find the story" as you're writing, you'll have to have some kind of outline for a branching story, *especially* if you're working with others. I'm not a big outliner and will jot down ideas for things that happen (but not necessarily when they happen) for nonchoice-based stories, but I would not be able to wrangle and keep track of choice points and what factors influence story progression if I didn't have a structured outline.

I have an initial outline for me and one for the team I'm working with. I work on the one for me first because I need to get a handle on the story myself before I can share the vision with anyone else. I first write things out in a notebook. I like to *feel* what I'm working on … something about the paper under my hand as it moves across the page and the ease of the pen flowing as I write … but I digress. I don't try to be perfect during this phase. All I'm trying to do now is to get down major plot points and character beats. I create several categories like "Main Plot" and "Character Development." I may start with a list of plot points but, as other ideas come to me, I end up writing character or subplot notes and worldbuilding info in the margins or squeezed above what I've already written on the line. Brainstorming and outlining tend to blur for me, so if new ideas come to me while I'm trying to outline, I don't want to self-edit.

As I work on the outline for the team, I type out everything I've written in my notebook. As I do so, I revise and refine my ideas, restructure and organize them, so they make sense for my audience. In doing so, I'm also cementing the structure and the concepts for the design in my own mind. I "learn" them in other words, and that helps me talk about the design with others and later write for it.

As I noted in "Writing for VN and Other Choice-Based Apps," your studio or client may give you an outlining format to work within. If it's not given to you, you'll have to develop a format for yourself. It may seem obvious to say so, but make sure your outline is easily readable and digestible:

- **Avoid Long Paragraphs:** A lot of devs I've met and worked with don't like to read. (This is not a judgment—just a fact.) Long paragraphs can be intimidating. Someone can look at a shorter paragraph at a glance and grasp the details.

- **Use Lots of White Space:** Shorter paragraphs and sentences surrounded by white space draw the eye.

- **Use Bullet Points:** Bullet points also draw the eye and emphasize information readers need to pay attention to.

TOOLS FOR OUTLINING

MICHELLE CLOUGH

Sometimes old school and simple is best for outlining branching, particularly when it's relatively simple. I have, on occasion, used simple Word or Google Docs documents with liberal use of bullet points, each bullet point being a particular conditional (e.g., "If you sided with X faction, this character is angry and rebuffs you. If you sided with Y faction they're friendly," etc.), or a particular outcome (e.g., "If you offer help, they welcome you. If you demand allegiance, they kick you out."). This format is particularly good for routes, quests, or storylines where the basic structure—or, at least, the beginning and the middle—remains mostly consistent (e.g., regardless of faction, you're always going to talk to this character, even if the outcome may change).

If you're outlining branching on a big macro level—where there may be a few massive major choices that lead to entirely different storylines, e.g., romance routes—this may also be a place where using hyperlinks and bookmarks within a Word or Google Docs document can be handy. You can break down the story chunks into paragraphs or pages and use hyperlinks to go between them. This format doesn't work as well for anything with tracked variables (e.g., certain items in inventory and character affection building) or with smaller micro choices, but it can be great for things like routes (romance or otherwise) or branching scenes that inevitably bottleneck back into a main storyline.

When I'm working with clients, another useful tool is Miro, which functions as an online whiteboard with sticky notes. This can be really handy for that "what info does the player need to know and when," as you can write them all out on sticky notes and then move them around as needed, under the appropriate sticky notes of the scenes themselves. Add in the ability to make flowcharts of those sticky notes, and it can be really handy for plotting out rough branching narrative, particularly when working with clients or collaborators live.

Lastly, while I haven't had a chance to really put it through its paces, consider articy:draft, particularly now that there's a free version. It has a branching tool for dialogue that can also be used for story outlines, and its multilayered design (e.g., having an object for, say, "Act 1" which can then be "zoomed into" for different objects for different scenes, each of which can be zoomed into again for the actual dialogue) offers a lot of possibility for robust outlining and, later, conversion to actual scripting, etc.

Designing When Players Unlock Content

You may have a general idea of content that you know players will be able to unlock in the game (like CGs), but you may have a larger list of types of unlockable content than you might first assume. Think of what's specific to your game and what players might feel is an achievement if they unlock it. For example, unlockable content specific to *Doki Doki Literature Club!* is the poetry the members of the club write over the course of the game. In *Monster Prom*, players unlock Polaroids after successful dates.

Make a list of the types of content that you might design as unlockables. Keep adding to it as things come to mind. Don't edit yourself at first. There will come a time when you'll have to make decisions about what does and doesn't go into the game, but don't limit your possibilities during the brainstorming process. Don't try to plan all of this first, although you may know what kind of content you want your players to unlock.

Possible Unlockables:

- CGs (computer graphics)
- Wallpapers
- Music
- Developmental art (character sketches, evolution of character designs, environments, etc.)
- Other game-specific content

CAPTION: *Monster Prom* Polaroids unlock during the end credits. Developed by Beautiful Glitch and protected by United States and international copyright law. © Beautiful Glitch.
"Vera Oberlin/Gallery," Monster Prom Wiki, accessed May 12, 2022, https://monster-prom.fandom.com/wiki/Vera_Oberlin/Gallery.

When you're ready to design what players unlock and where, think about when unlocking the content would make sense. Character routes, the moments players unlock CGs in the game, etc.

PROCESSES

Prototyping

By prototyping, you can design one or more scenes, the entire main story, or routes, and play them. This doesn't mean that you have all narrative, dialogue, and choices in place, but you have the barebones structure of how the game will play. This is useful because you can tell if certain routes are too long or short. You can test how satisfying choices feel, and you can find continuity errors or places where you didn't rejoin branches to the main story.

Narrative scripting languages like Twine, ink, and Yarn Spinner can get prototypes up and running quickly, and you can play these prototypes.

Sticky Notes and Paper Connected by String

Twine simulates the technique of placing sticky notes on a wall or table or placing paper/note cards on a corkboard and connecting them with string. Having a more physical prototype with sticky notes means you can be hands on with the design. You're able to see everything in front of you, and you can move around notes, add more notes, and remove notes as you iterate on your design.

Slide Prototypes

It might seem a little strange but, yes, you *can* simulate story progressions through a slide deck using programs like PowerPoint or Google Slides. You can make slides interactive and link slides through choices or words on the slides.[3] You might only have text on the slides, or you might add images as references to communicate your user interface (UI), text boxes, buttons, and other design ideas for screens, or you might even use concept art produced for the game.

And if you haven't learned a narrative scripting language and don't have the time to learn before you have to produce a prototype, you can use PowerPoint or Google Slides as an effective method.

OUTLINING AND PROTOTYPING IN TWINE IN DETAIL

MICHELLE CLOUGH

Twine is definitely one of my go-to choices for outlining intricate branching, either for a particular scene or for an entire story. What I will often do is what I call a "placeholder" Twine that works as both an outline and a sort of prototype.

- I begin the Twine file with a series of questions about larger story dependencies that might affect the scene or storyline I'm trying to outline. For example, if the game has an earlier scene where you could help an old lady across a raging river, and then I'm working on outlining a scene where you meet the old lady again, I'd start off with a game state question like, "Did you help the old lady over the river in the earlier scene?", then make sure that gets marked down as a Boolean[4] that can/will then be used in the scene outline.

- If and when that previous state comes into play, you can use conditionals and the display to indicate what happens and what the impact is. For example, "Because you helped the little old lady, she's already well disposed to you! +10 to Old Lady Respect."

- As I write the story, I state or summarize very clearly what happens in each "node" of the story. For example, "The player is lost in the forest and wandering in the moonlight when they meet someone. It's the old lady!" Any player choices are also similarly summed up in a clear, concise manner—it doesn't have to be specific and can sometimes be literally placeholders (e.g., "Greeting option," "Suspicious option"), but they give enough context to get a sense of what the choices are.

- For every node, or at least every node in which a variable is changed, increased, decreased, etc., show the variables in question at the top and indicate they're being changed. For example, if players take the "Greeting option," the next node might start with "Old Lady Respect has gone up by 1! Old Lady Respect currently at [current value]."

- For conditional routes, things that either depend on a particular variable value being high enough (e.g., Old Lady Respect), or on a particular choice or action (e.g., did you help the old lady cross the river?), use <display> to show a link to the resulting outcome with a clearly written statement of why the outcome is happening. For example, if there's a specific scene that plays if the Old Lady's respect is higher than 10, use that conditional to display a link that says, "If the Old Lady's respect is high enough/over 10 …," clicking the link then takes you to the scene in question.

- At the end of the outline, have a sum-up of all variables, choices, and major branches to review what happened and why, and make sure all your states and variables were tracked consistently (e.g., "You got 15 Old Lady Respect! The Old Lady liked you and showed you where she hid her treasure.").

The result of doing this is a simple yet robust playable prototype, one that lets you playtest easily without having to write out the whole thing, and which makes it easier to see possible branching spots or conditionals that you may have missed. Added bonus, you could theoretically take it and flesh it out into a fully written scene!

Designing Flowcharts and Wireframes
Sketching

There are several flowchart and diagramming programs available now, but sometimes it's easier to help you visualize the story's flow if you sketch it out for yourself first. You can then go into a program and design the flowchart, or somebody on your team might take your drawings and design the flowchart/diagram.

If you're not the artist and you feel comfortable drawing, you might sketch some of your ideas in pictorial form to help yourself get a better sense of how characters might interact with each other, what some of the action scenes might be, or how the main character (MC) might explore the environment. Your sketches will also be great references for artists.

Designing Screen Flow

As I mentioned under "Slide Prototypes," you can place images on slides to give an idea of how you want screens to look. You can also design concepts for how players will interact with screens and menus. In the screen flow, you diagram what happens when players interact with elements on the screen (like the help menu pops up when they click on the help button or choice buttons pop up after clicking on the text box). Wireframing tools like Miro, draw.io, Google Drawings, and Figma are useful for this. You can also do this through slides.

SOME FINAL WORDS OF ENCOURAGEMENT

There's a lot to unpack here if you've never used these tools, and you don't even know where to start. Brains work differently, we have different learning styles, and something I can learn easily might be difficult for you, and vice versa. If you're not sure where to begin at any part of the planning, design, or writing process, chat with friends who've worked on choice-based games. Or search places like Twitter for conversations about tools or processes. You'll get more insight into what devs see as strengths and weaknesses with these techniques and tools and what might or might not work for you.

I also don't want to suggest that working on a visual novel (or any game) is *easy*. Making any game is hard, even when you're participating in a 2- or 3-day game jam. But the challenge of designing and writing the game is going to surprise you in some fun ways. You're going to come up with some cool answers to problems. The team you collaborate with is going to inspire each other, and the story that results is going to be far beyond what you visualized before you put pen to paper or typed in a word processor.

As I mentioned in "Choice-Based Games and Visual Novels," VNs give you a lot of flexibility to play in story settings and experiment with mechanics. There *is* an audience out there that's waiting to play your game.

NOTES

1 Visual coders (or visual programming languages) allow you to do all of the programming through a graphical interface instead of typing in the code.
2 I found Fungus very easy to learn, and I scripted *Vanished* in it. I learned Fungus in a day and a half, and then worked on *Vanished* that weekend for Global Game Jam.
3 Searching online for tutorials on making choice-based or interactive stories in PowerPoint or Google Slides will bring up a number of tutorials.
4 A Boolean is a type of data that only has two values: true or false.

Index

Note: *Italic* page numbers refer to figures

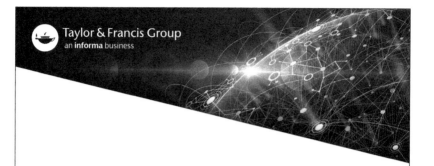

Taylor & Francis Group
an **informa** business

Taylor & Francis eBooks

www.taylorfrancis.com

A single destination for eBooks from Taylor & Francis
with increased functionality and an improved user
experience to meet the needs of our customers.

90,000+ eBooks of award-winning academic content in
Humanities, Social Science, Science, Technology, Engineering,
and Medical written by a global network of editors and authors.

TAYLOR & FRANCIS EBOOKS OFFERS:

A streamlined
experience for
our library
customers

A single point
of discovery
for all of our
eBook content

Improved
search and
discovery of
content at both
book and
chapter level

REQUEST A FREE TRIAL
support@taylorfrancis.com

Routledge
Taylor & Francis Group

CRC Press
Taylor & Francis Group

9781032059006